THE MAGNITSKY ACT AT FIVE YEARS:
ASSESSING ACCOMPLISHMENTS AND CHALLENGES

HEARING

BEFORE THE

COMMISSION ON SECURITY AND COOPERATION IN EUROPE

ONE HUNDRED FIFTEENTH CONGRESS

FIRST SESSION

DECEMBER 14, 2017

Printed for the use of the
Commission on Security and Cooperation in Europe

[CSCE 115–1–7]

Available via www.csce.gov

U.S. GOVERNMENT PUBLISHING OFFICE

28–314PDF   WASHINGTON : 2018

For sale by the Superintendent of Documents, U.S. Government Publishing Office
Internet: bookstore.gpo.gov   Phone: toll free (866) 512–1800; DC area (202) 512–1800
Fax: (202) 512–2104   Mail: Stop IDCC, Washington, DC 20402–0001

COMMISSION ON SECURITY AND COOPERATION IN EUROPE

LEGISLATIVE BRANCH COMMISSIONERS

HOUSE	SENATE
CHRISTOPHER H. SMITH, New Jersey, *Co-Chairman*	ROGER F. WICKER, Mississippi, *Chairman*
ALCEE L. HASTINGS, Florida	BENJAMIN L. CARDIN, Maryland
ROBERT B. ADERHOLT, Alabama	JOHN BOOZMAN, Arkansas
MICHAEL C. BURGESS, Texas	CORY GARDNER, Colorado
STEVE COHEN, Tennessee	MARCO RUBIO, Florida
RICHARD HUDSON, North Carolina	JEANNE SHAHEEN, New Hampshire
RANDY HULTGREN, Illinois	THOM TILLIS, North Carolina
SHEILA JACKSON LEE, Texas	TOM UDALL, New Mexico
GWEN MOORE, Wisconsin	SHELDON WHITEHOUSE, Rhode Island

EXECUTIVE BRANCH COMMISSIONERS

Vacant, Department of State
Vacant, Department of Commerce
Vacant, Department of Defense

[II]

THE MAGNITSKY ACT AT FIVE YEARS: ASSESSING ACCOMPLISHMENTS AND CHALLENGES

DECEMBER 14, 2017

COMMISSIONERS

COMMISSION STAFF

WITNESSES

APPENDICES

IV

THE MAGNITSKY ACT AT FIVE YEARS: ASSESSING ACCOMPLISHMENTS AND CHALLENGES

December 14, 2017

COMMISSION ON SECURITY AND COOPERATION IN EUROPE

WASHINGTON, DC

The hearing was held at 9:36 a.m. in Room 562, Dirksen Senate Office Building, Washington, DC, Hon. Roger Wicker, Chairman, Commission on Security and Cooperation in Europe, presiding.

Commissioners present: Hon. Roger Wicker, Chairman, Commission on Security and Cooperation in Europe; Hon. Benjamin Cardin, Ranking Member, Commission on Security and Cooperation in Europe; Hon. Christopher Smith, Co-Chairman, Commission on Security and Cooperation in Europe; Hon. Steven Cohen, Commissioner, Commission on Security and Cooperation in Europe; Hon. Gwen Moore, Commissioner, Commission on Security and Cooperation in Europe; Hon. Sheldon Whitehouse, Commissioner, Commission on Security and Cooperation in Europe; Hon. Cory Gardner, Commissioner, Commission on Security and Cooperation in Europe; Hon. Sheila Jackson Lee, Commissioner, Commission on Security and Cooperation in Europe; and Hon. Jeanne Shaheen, Commissioner, Commission on Security and Cooperation in Europe.

Commission staff present: Ambassador David T. Killion, Chief of Staff, Commission on Security and Cooperation in Europe.

Witnesses present: William Browder, CEO, Hermitage Capital Management; Garry Kasparov, Chairman, Human Rights Foundation; and Irwin Cotler, PC, OC, Chair, Raoul Wallenberg Center for Human Rights.

HON. ROGER WICKER, CHAIRMAN, COMMISSION ON SECURITY AND COOPERATION IN EUROPE

Mr. WICKER. [Sounds gavel.] The hearing of the Commission will come to order, and good morning to all of you. Welcome to today's hearing on "The Magnitsky Act at Five Years: Assessing Accomplishments and Challenges."

Before we begin today, I want to recognize Ambassador David Killion.

AMBASSADOR DAVID T. KILLION, CHIEF OF STAFF, COMMISSION ON SECURITY AND COOPERATION IN EUROPE

Amb. KILLION. Right here, Senator.

Mr. WICKER. Just stand for a moment. Thank you. Thank you, David—the Helsinki Commission Chief of Staff who is retiring at the end of this month after 23 years of federal service. Senator Cardin and I joined together to appoint Ambassador Killion to direct the Commission at a key moment, shortly after Russia's invasion of Crimea in 2014. So let's give Ambassador Killion a round of applause. [Applause.]

Ambassador Killion's leadership has contributed greatly to enhancing the stature and impact of our Commission as it develops U.S. policy responses to critical security threats in the OSCE region. With his considerable diplomatic skills, he has also managed to keep our Commission unified, enabling us to speak with a strong voice when necessary on issues such as Russia's violation of its Helsinki commitments. In addition, Ambassador Killion has extended Commission leadership to new and critically relevant policy areas such as the effort to combat kleptocracy. As such, this hearing is a perfect capstone to Ambassador Killion's work for us.

Ambassador, thank you for your public service.

This is the Commission's final hearing of 2017.

HON. BENJAMIN CARDIN, RANKING MEMBER, COMMISSION ON SECURITY AND COOPERATION IN EUROPE

Mr. CARDIN. Mr. Chairman, on Ambassador Killion—if I could, just for one moment—I really want to join you in thanking Ambassador Killion for his service to the Helsinki Commission and to our country. He had a distinguished career as an ambassador to UNESCO and brought that talent to the Helsinki Commission. What we really love about this Commission and its work, it's never been partisan. It's been professional. And Mr. Killion has continued that legacy during extremely difficult, turbulent times.

I want to thank him for his service to our country, thank him for his service to this Commission, and wish him well.

Amb. KILLION. Thank you.

Mr. WICKER. Thank you, Senator Cardin. And I'm sure you have expressed the feelings of us all.

The Magnitsky Act was authored by Senator McCain, Senator Cardin, and me to hold accountable the Russians who were responsible for the torture and murder of tax attorney Sergei Magnitsky in 2012. Why was the Helsinki Commission concerned about this particular crime? The mandate of the Helsinki Commission requires us to monitor the acts of the signatories which reflect compliance with or violation of the articles of the Final Act of the Conference on Security and Cooperation in Europe, also known as the Helsinki Final Act. Those articles deal with commitments in three major areas, or baskets: security, economics, and the human dimension. The case that ended with Sergei Magnitsky's tragic death concerned major violations in two of these three baskets: massive corruption in Russia, which the OSCE attempts to deal with through economic measures, and the egregious human rights violations involved in the unspeakable treatment of Sergei Magnitsky.

The five years that have elapsed since the passage of the Magnitsky Act and the eight years that have elapsed since Mr. Magnitsky's murder have certainly shown that our concern with Russia's unchecked corruption and wanton disregard for human rights was well founded. In that time corruption has continued to eat away at the fabric of Russian society, enabling further mis-behavior both within and beyond Russia's borders. The state at this point can truly be described as a kleptocracy, where Putin rules with the help of a group of cronies whose loyalty is guaranteed by transfers of wealth stolen from the Russian people. Russia has vio-lated the territorial integrity of a European state and interfered with the elections of a number of OSCE participating States, in-cluding the United States. And, of course, Russian citizens continue to suffer from the policies of their own government on a daily basis.

Russian opposition leader Boris Nemtsov, who was himself mur-dered in 2015 within sight of the Kremlin walls, deemed the Magnitsky Act, quote, "the most pro-Russia law for justice." We do sincerely hope that the Magnitsky Act will one day lead to justice, not only for Sergei Magnitsky and his family and friends, but also for all Russians who suffer violations of their universal rights by a state that believes it is accountable to no one.

We have three remarkable witnesses to speak to us today about what the Magnitsky Act has accomplished, as well as what still needs to be done to encourage Russia to respect the rights of its citizens and live up to its OSCE commitments.

We will first hear from William Browder, the CEO of Hermitage Capital, the firm that was plundered to the tune of $230 million in a massive tax-evasion scheme by Russian authorities. Mr. Browder has worked tirelessly for the past eight years, at great risk to his own safety, to bring those responsible for Sergei Magnitsky's murder to justice. I strongly encourage any of you who have not read the book "Red Notice" to do so. It is a gripping and unforgettable account of massive corruption, torture, and murder with impunity.

After that, Garry Kasparov will provide us with a broader view, addressing the full scale of corruption and human rights violations in Russia. Mr. Kasparov is well known to most of us as one of the greatest chess players in history, becoming the youngest world champion ever at age 22 in 1985. He's now 32, I believe. [Laugh-ter.] But I don't count very well. After 20 years at the top of the chess world, he gave it up and joined the fledgling Russia pro-democracy movement in 2005. He participated, along with Boris Nemtsov, in the May 2012 Bolotnaya Square demonstrations, one of the biggest protests held in Russia since the 1990s. These pro-tests were followed by an extensive crackdown that forced him to leave the country and relocate to New York. Mr. Kasparov is the chairman of the New York-based Human Rights Foundation, and he has also found the time to write a book entitled "Winter is Com-ing: Why Putin and Enemies of the Free World Must Be Stopped."

And then we will hear from Honorable Professor Irwin Cotler, who will testify about his work to pass a Canadian version of the Magnitsky Act. The pressure from Russia on Mr. Cotler and other Canadian backers of that bill has been immense, just as it has been in every other country that has considered passing a version of the Magnitsky Act. Professor Cotler has a distinguished career in advancing human rights around the world, not only as Canada's attorney general and justice minister, but also as founder and chair of the Raoul Wallenberg Center, an institution dedicated to bringing together all parts of civil society in the defense of human rights.

And so we welcome our panel. And before we proceed to testimony, I'd like to ask my distinguished Co-Chair, Mr. Smith of New Jersey, if he would like to make any remarks.

HON. CHRIS SMITH, CO-CHAIRMAN, COMMISSION ON SECURITY AND COOPERATION IN EUROPE

Mr. SMITH. Thank you, Mr. Chairman.

First of all, I want to join you in thanking Ambassador Killion for his service to the Commission. He served as ambassador to UNESCO, where pervasive and systematic anti-Semitism abounds to this very day, and he did a valiant fight against those other ambassadors and those other countries. And I want to thank him for that.

And I've known David since he was on the Foreign Affairs Committee, working with Tom Lantos, so I want to thank him for his service to our country and to the Commission. Thank you, David.

Thank you, Mr. Chairman, for convening this very important hearing on the fifth anniversary of the Sergei Magnitsky Rule of Law Accountability Act. This all began with Sergei Magnitsky's investigation into the brazen theft of $230 million from the Russian people by officers of FSB Unit K in the Interior Ministry. Sergei continued to expose Colonel Kuznetsov and Major Karpov's plunder from foreign investors, and documented how they lavishly spent it while millions of Russians struggled to get by. For that, Kuznetsov and Karpov illegally detained Sergei, repeatedly tortured him, and denied him medical attention, all in the hope that they could force him to confess and absolve themselves of their crimes. Sergei was murdered because he would never confess to trumped-up charges and never gave in to the brutality. Kuznetsov and Karpov were only two out of 60 Russians that were determined to be involved in this horrific crime and its coverup.

Congress passed the Sergei Magnitsky Act five years ago to ensure that Sergei and his family got the justice they deserved—at least a modicum of justice—and to send a message to Russia that this will not stand. The identification and sanction of those involved in all aspects of Sergei's illegal detention, torture, and murder struck right to the heart of the Kremlin's elite. It sent an unmistakable signal that the United States of America is prepared to sanction all those involved in human rights abuses in Russia.

In response, President Putin took his wrath out on innocent Russian orphans who had been destined to be adopted by American families. And I've met with many of them, as have many of my colleagues. Some of those kids in Russia were in need of serious medical attention, and their hopes of a loving family and a happier life were dashed, all because the cynical Kremlin elite saw harming vulnerable children as the best means to retaliate against the United States.

Putin, still reeling from the impact of the Magnitsky Act, lashed out at the U.S. Government and at many of us on this Commission and in the House and the Senate. I was denied a visa when I tried to do a trip on Magnitsky and also on human trafficking, as the OSCE special representative for trafficking. Russia has a huge problem with trafficking, particularly of women into sex trafficking. And I met with their ambassador, and I was denied and was told the reason was the Magnitsky Act.

I would point out parenthetically that during the worst days of communism, at least when I was in Congress—I got elected in 1980, took office in 1981—I went in 1982 with the National Conference on Soviet Jewry. They didn't want us there. We spent 10 days in Moscow and Leningrad, met with refuseniks including Sharansky's mother, but we got visas. The same thing happened when Frank Wolf and I went to Perm Camp 35 just a few years later. We got into the infamous Perm Camp where Sharansky and many other political and refuseniks and others had spent time, thousands of miles outside of Moscow in the Ural Mountains. But we got visas. But because of the Magnitsky Act, this penalty, this punitive action has denied many of us visas to go there to raise human rights issues face to face with the Kremlin elite.

So I want to thank you, Mr. Chairman, for convening this important hearing. I have to point out at 10:00 we have a markup on four bills in the Foreign Affairs Committee. I have to speak on two of them, so I will have to leave. But I wanted to know the three distinguished witnesses who are here in our room—Irwin, we worked so long and hard on combating anti-Semitism—and thank you for your great leadership there as well.

And, again, Mr. Chairman, I'm sorry to have to go.

Mr. WICKER. Thank you very much, Representative Smith.

Senator Cardin.

Mr. CARDIN. Well, Chairman Wicker, first of all, thank you for your leadership on the Helsinki Commission. You have been a true champion on the human rights basket of the OSCE and the U.S. participation, and I thank you for convening this hearing.

We do have three very distinguished witnesses here today, and we thank all three for being here.

Mr. Browder, I remember when you first brought Sergei Magnitsky to my attention in June of 2009, and I was shocked to hear what had happened. And you were able to do something that has been very difficult. What happened to Sergei Magnitsky was not unique under Mr. Putin in Russia, but what made it unique was your ability to tell that story to the international community. And the international community was forced to take action, and you were able to take that activity to help so many people around the world. So I thank you for your courage, and I thank you for making sure that we remember Sergei Magnitsky, remember his courage, and are motivated by him every day.

To Mr. Cotler, I want to thank you. Canada has been our true ally and friend because there was a lot of pushback about taking action against Russia, and your leadership in Canada, your leadership in helping us with the OSCE Parliamentary Assembly was critical. And we thank you for that partnership, for giving us international legitimacy to moving forward on the Magnitsky Act.

And, Mr. Kasparov, I want to thank you because you represent the Russian people, what the Russian people want. This is not about penalizing Russia. It's about penalizing the leaders of Russia for what they're doing, and first hurting the people of their own country.

So I thank our three witnesses.

The tragic death of Sergei Magnitsky in November 2009 for discovering $230 million of corruption, one of the largest in the history of Russia, was just beyond our comprehension, that the political leadership of Russia could stoop to that type of level and take out the life of a very young lawyer. And we took some action. We, the Helsinki Commission, said, look, we're going to do some things.

And I remember conversations I had with the administration on how we could perhaps use the visas or use the banking system to take action against the known perpetrators, and those conversations were going through the normal bureaucracy problems that you see in the executive branch and in diplomacy. So, in April of 2010, I sent a letter to Secretary of State Clinton suggesting formally that she take action. And they were considering it.

And then, Mr. Chairman, we came to the conclusion that for this to really work—we knew the executive had the authority, but would they exercise that authority? Because when you talk about bilateral relations with countries, there's so many things on the agenda; will human rights really get the place it needs? So we knew that Congress needed to act.

And the Helsinki Commission did get engaged on this issue. I filed legislation, and I was proud of so many people who joined in that. And I thank the Chairman, Senator Wicker. Clearly, Senator McCain was one of our true champions through this process, and our prayers are with him on his health as we go through this. I also want to mention Kyle Parker, a staff member of the Helsinki Commission who was critically important in keeping us focused. And, again, this never became partisan, and we worked it through the Senate.

I then went on the Senate Foreign Relations Committee and got a little bit of a hostile treatment there. But a champion emerged, and I have to mention that. Senator Lugar was a real champion in giving us, again, the bipartisan support. Senator Shaheen was a critical supporter on the Senate Foreign Relations on this issue. And we got it enacted, and we celebrate the fifth anniversary of its enactment.

But we didn't stop there, because it was Russia-specific and we knew that these problems are global. And last year we passed the Global Magnitsky Act.

I just really want to acknowledge that when we lead, we find other countries that follow. And with Canada and U.S. leadership, we've seen action taken in Estonia, in Lithuania, in U.K., and we've made significant progress.

So I just really want to acknowledge the importance of the work that has been done, but as I said earlier, we can't rest on our laurels. There are serious issues globally taking place. The administration is supposed to present their Global Magnitsky list very shortly, and we'll be watching that very closely. We also will be watching their implementation of the Russian sanction law. That requires reports as early as next month, and we'll be watching very closely to make sure they comply with the laws that we have passed.

The bottom line is that the Helsinki Commission and the United States Congress have taken leadership on this issue, and we will continue to lead on protecting human rights globally.

Mr. WICKER. Thank you very much. And let me note at this point that other representatives and senators may have statements that they can enter into the record at this point.

But right now we are eager to hear our witnesses. And, Mr. Browder, you are recognized for such time as you may consume. Thank you.

WILLIAM BROWDER, CEO, HERMITAGE CAPITAL MANAGEMENT

Mr. BROWDER. Good morning, Chairman Wicker, Ranking Member Cardin, Co-Chair Smith. Thank you very much for the opportunity to come here and to testify on the fifth anniversary of the passage of the Magnitsky Act.

I could have never imagined on the 17th of November, 2009, the day that I learned that Sergei Magnitsky had been murdered, that three years later the most important piece of human rights legislation of this century would come into force in the United States and be name after Sergei Magnitsky.

And on December 14th, 2012, five years ago today, when the Magnitsky Act was passed, I could have never imagined that the Magnitsky movement would emerge from the work that started here, that would lead to five countries now having the Magnitsky Act in place and many more with it on the agenda. We truly have a global movement.

And I should emphasize that this global movement started right here. It started with the Helsinki Commission. It started first with a staff meeting. I had a staff meeting with Kyle Parker—whom I guess you will recognize as now being your new chief of staff shortly—in which I told the story of Sergei Magnitsky. And this was actually in 2009, before Sergei Magnitsky had died. It was while he was still alive and in prison. And Kyle was so shocked by the story he said, I think we should invite you to a Helsinki Commission hearing.

And it was at that moment that I met Senator Cardin. And Senator Cardin heard the story while Sergei Magnitsky was still alive. And because he heard this shocking story of injustice and corruption while Sergei was still alive, when Sergei was murdered, Senator Cardin was the first leader on the scene to do something about it. And Senator Cardin introduced, in October of 2010, together with Senator Wicker, Senator McCain, and Senator Lieberman, the Sergei Magnitsky Act.

The Sergei Magnitsky Act was, as you have pointed out, something where we then had Garry Kasparov and Boris Nemtsov and various others coming and saying, this is not an anti-Russian piece of legislation, this is a pro-Russian piece of legislation, and it took on great resonance as other victims came forward. And in spite of the fact that at the time the U.S. administration was trying to reset relations with Russia, this was one of the moments in Washington where morality overcame realpolitik, and when it came for a vote in the Senate it passed 92 to 4, as you know, it passed 89 percent of the House of Representatives, and it was signed into law.

And I'm happy to be sitting here with you today knowing that you decided not to stop with just that, but to take it globally. And Senator Cardin, Senator Wicker, Senator McCain then introduced the Global Magnitsky Act in 2015. And in spite of fierce, aggressive opposition by the Russian Government—and the Russian Government did not want to have the Magnitsky legacy on the Global Magnitsky Act, and Natalia Veselnitskaya, the famous lobbyist, showed up here in the halls of Congress with highly paid lobbyists and lawyers and PR firms trying to take the Magnitsky name off of that piece of legislation. They went to Trump Tower to talk about this legislation. But in spite of their great efforts, the Global Magnitsky Act passed.

On roughly the same day as Global Magnitsky passed in 2016, the Estonians—a little country in the Baltics, right on the border of Russia—passed their Magnitsky Act. And then the U.K., the country where I live and where I'm a citizen, passed the Magnitsky Act in May of this year.

And I'm particularly proud to be sitting here with Irwin Cotler. Irwin Cotler is the father of the Magnitsky Act in Canada. As Senator Cardin is to the Magnitsky Act in America, Irwin Cotler is to the Magnitsky Act in Canada. I went to Irwin in 2010. And it took us a little longer; it took us seven years. But I actually had tears running down my face when I watched the Parliament voting 277 to zero in favor of the Canadian Magnitsky Act. And it was even more moving when I brought the Magnitsky family to the Canadian Parliament a few weeks later, and the Parliament stood up and gave the family a two-minute standing ovation for the sacrifice that Sergei had made.

And then, on the eighth anniversary of Sergei's murder, the Lithuanian parliament voted 71 to zero, and the Lithuanians passed it.

There are now a number of countries that are teeing up the Magnitsky Act. Ukraine is going to introduce a Magnitsky Act. Gibraltar, without any intervention from any activists, have introduced their version of the Magnitsky Act. The South African Parliament will be introducing a Magnitsky Act. And there are many, many others.

As you can imagine, Putin has been not too happy about this, and I've paid a high personal price for this. After the U.S. Magnitsky Act was passed, I was put on trial, together with Sergei Magnitsky, in the first-ever trial against a dead man in the history of Russia. They sentenced me to nine years in absentia to serve in a Russian prison colony. Afterwards, they have applied to Interpol five times to have me arrested on an Interpol arrest warrant. The most recent application came right after the Canadian act was passed. Fortunately, Interpol has rejected all five requests. The Russians have approached the British Government on 12 different occasions asking for mutual legal assistance and extradition. Thankfully, the British Government has rejected all those requests.

But the Russians don't give up. They've since accused me of serial murder. They've accused me of murdering Sergei Magnitsky. They've accused me of espionage, of being a CIA/MI6 agent trying to destabilize Russia. They've accused me of stealing $4.8 billion from the IMF. They've accused me of tax evasion, fraud, and many other things.

They've not stopped with just legal nastiness. They've also threatened to kill me. They have threatened to kidnap me. They, of course, tried to arrest me, and various other things.

But I'm not stopping. I'm not stopping, and nor should you.

And so there are four things that we still need to do that are on my list. The first is that, while we have a Magnitsky Act, the Magnitsky list is incomplete. There are 44 people on the Magnitsky list so far; 35 of them are involved in the Magnitsky case. We submitted 282 names to the State Department, and those many other unsanctioned people need to be sanctioned.

The second thing is that people have learned to evade Magnitsky sanctions. There's a man named Dmitry Klyuev, who is on the Magnitsky list. Dmitry Klyuev is the head of the Klyuev organized crime group. And Dmitry Klyuev, shortly before being put on the Magnitsky list, moved all his assets into the names of nominees. I presented that information to the U.S. Treasury to say that he and his nominees are in violation of U.S. sanctions. So far, no action has been taken.

And it's not just Klyuev, but the entire concept of Bitcoin and cryptocurrencies are a way to avoid Magnitsky sanctions and all other sanctions. And this is a huge issue that needs to be addressed going forward, because while these sanctions have worked in the past, they won't work in the future if people can move money anonymously around the world.

And then, finally, there is one provision in the Magnitsky Act which most people don't know about, which I want to bring to your attention, which is that it's also the U.S. Government's responsibility to advocate for Magnitsky Acts in other countries. It's in the law. At the moment, it's been used informally, and I'd like to ask you to promote the idea that the government formalizes its advocacy in other countries. And the best place to do that will be at the G-7 meeting in June in Canada. At the G-7 meeting there will be three countries of the G-97—the United States, Canada, and the United Kingdom—that all have Magnitsky Acts, and there are four other countries that don't. And it should be a U.S. official policy, together with the Canadians and the U.K., to promote it among our allies at the G-7.

I should say that all of this stuff has happened because of the great work of your Commission and the great work of my colleagues here on the panel and other people. But it also has happened because Sergei's story is biblical in its good versus evil. And I hope that you will carry on in this campaign for justice in this moment for Sergei Magnitsky.

Thank you very much.

Mr. WICKER. Thank you very much, Mr. Browder.

Mr. Kasparov, you're recognized.

GARRY KASPAROV, CHAIRMAN, HUMAN RIGHTS FOUNDATION

Mr. KASPAROV. Thank you for having me here today, and to Chairman Wicker and Co-Chairman Smith and Ranking Member Cardin for holding these hearings on a topic of vital national and international security.

I will understand if few of you recall that I spoke here over 13 years ago, in May 2004, on a panel titled "Human Rights in Putin's Russia." At the time, Bill Browder and I were still attempting to do our part to salvage democracy and the rule of law from inside Putin's Russia, while the entire democratic world preferred to ignore the true nature of what Putin was doing in my country.

Mikhail Khodorkovsky had just been arrested. There were still a dwindling handful of Russian media not under direct Kremlin control. The Russian Parliament still had a few members who would occasionally criticize Putin. Anna Politkovskaya, and Boris Nemtsov, Sergei Magnitsky, and so many others who opposed Putin were all still alive.

I am not the sort of person to wallow in nostalgia, but it's hard not to think of how different Russia and the world might be today had the free world taken a stand against Vladimir Putin back then, before he had consolidated total power in Russia. In 2004, Putin still needed friends on the international stage, and he had many of them. By 2012 that phase was over, and a far deadlier phase of dictatorship began, when Putin needed not friends, but external enemies to justify his eternal grip on power. Today, there is no longer any need to discuss human rights in Putin's Russia. They are gone, and Putin is revealed to all as what we warned he could become: a dictator.

And please do not speak of Putin's supposed popularity. A popular leader does not need to fake elections, or destroy the free media, or jail critics and kill opposition leaders. Status that is artificially fashioned by 24/7 propaganda, repression of all dissent, and the elimination of all rivals is not approval, it is dictatorship.

Here, 13 years ago, I said: "Without Western attention and pressure, the situation will only worsen during Putin's next four years." We still dreamed that Putin could be forced to hold real elections in 2008, but it was not to be. Later I said: "Putin is a Russian problem, for Russians to deal with. But if he isn't stopped, he will soon be a regional problem—and after, he will be everyone's problem."

Fast-forward to 2006 and the murder of Russian anti-Putin whistleblower Alexander Litvinenko in London with a nuclear isotope; 2008, and Putin's invasion of Georgia, for which he also suffered no consequences and was even rewarded with the infamous American "reset." Jump to 2012 and Putin's broad crackdown against any and all opposition and demonstrations, which led to Boris Nemtsov's murder and my own exile; to 2014 and Putin's invasion of Crimea and eastern Ukraine; to 2016 and direct Russian interference in the American presidential elections after similar activities in the U.K., Netherlands, and elsewhere in Europe.

Natan Sharansky quotes Andrei Sakharov saying: "The country that doesn't respect the rights of its own people will not respect the rights of its neighbors." And as the United States discovered last year, in the age of internet we are all neighbors.

For a decade now, many of us familiar with the reality of Putin and his regime, including both of my fellow guests here to offer testimony, have insisted that the only effective way to pressure Putin is to target the only thing he cares about: his hold on power in Russia. And that the best way to target Putin's power is to take aim at his agents and cronies and their money, to pursue the mafia

that holds the levers of power and who benefit the most from
Putin's rule. The individuals who can influence Putin must be targeted or there can be no effective deterrence.

There is no national Russian interest Putin cares about beyond
propaganda value. In fact, Russian national interest and Putin's interests are diametrically opposed in nearly every way. Putin does
not care about the Russian people, the Russian economy, or the
image of Russia abroad. I repeat: He does not care. This is why legislation that targets Putin and his mafia is pro-Russia, not anti-
Russia. A strong, free, and democratic Russia would be an ally of
the West, and that can never happen under Putin.

But I know that first and foremost we are here to discuss the interests of the United States—its security, integrity, and economic
well being. Consider the American and other free world policy goals
of dealing with Putin's aggression. One, to improve American and
international security by deterring him from further hostile acts.
Ukraine, Syria, Venezuela, missile tech to North Korea, election
meddling—Putin's attacks are asymmetric, and so the global response must be asymmetric as well, by going after what matters
to him most. Two, to threaten Putin's grasp on total power in Russia by forcing his elites to choose between loyalty to him and their
fortunes abroad. Three, to support the long-term interests of the
Russian people by exposing the corruption of our rulers. To all
three of these goals, the Magnitsky Act is the answer.

Putin's regime is a mafia, and you have to fight it like a mafia.
Very strong penalties must be ready and widely known. I understand that deterrence is difficult because its fruits are not apparent. If it works, maybe nothing visible happens. To those who say
that sanctions have not worked, can you say what else Putin might
have done without them in place, or why he works so frantically
to have them repealed?

Progress in a hybrid war is not measured in territory conquered
or battlefield casualties. Corrupting influence and propaganda
spread like contagious diseases. You can measure the effectiveness
of the Magnitsky legislation the way you measure the effectiveness
of antibiotics: You put a drop in the petri dish and see if the bacteria stop growing, if the bacteria respond to the antibiotic and die.
By this measure, the Magnitsky Act has been effective, and could
be much more effective if strengthened and implemented globally
and aggressively.

Last month, a Reuters report said anxiety was spreading among
Russia's wealthiest because of sanctions and the threat of the U.S.
blacklist. It reported that some business leaders were trying to
avoid being seen in public near Putin and to distance themselves.
This is progress. It shows the medicine is effective. But anxiety is
not enough to turn someone against a brutal dictator. Avoiding
photo-ops is not enough to bring down a mafia. It's essential to increase the pressure, to continue with what works now that the
right path has been confirmed. There is no other method.

Putin's weapons of hybrid war can only be defended against at
great difficulty and expense. Misinformation, cyberwarfare, and his
other methods are cheap and easy to deploy. And to take it from
a pretty good chess player, playing only defense is always a losing
game. The answer is deterrence. Putin and his gang must under-

stand that if he continues on this path, their fortunes, their families' comfortable lives abroad, will be at risk. They aren't really politicians, nor are they jihadists or ideologues. They are billionaires who are used to profiting from dictatorship at home while enjoying the good life in the West, an advantage the Soviet leaders never had.

This is increasingly true of other hostile regimes around the world: Small groups of ruling elites who do not care about traditional national interests and diplomatic levers of power because they are only interested in their personal success. Engagement does not work with them. Diplomacy doesn't, either. Magnitsky legislation does.

End the perverse double standards. Follow the money, the real estate, the stock, and reveal it, freeze it, so that one day it can be returned to the people from whom it was looted, and to help rebuild the countries that have been drained for so long. In Russia's case, the brittle nature of Putin's one-man dictatorship will be exposed very quickly.

At a lecture in New York City in 1975, my Russian predecessor-in-exile Aleksandr Solzhenitsyn said, "The men who created your country never lost sight of their moral bearings. Their practical policies were checked against that moral compass. A practical policy on the basis of moral considerations turned out to be the most farsighted and most salutary." That is, the most moral policy turns out to be the most effective policy.

The alternative to appeasement is not war, it is deterrence. And worrying about retaliation is absurd when Putin will continue to escalate anyway, as long as he thinks he can get away with it. The best way to avoid an escalating conflict is to convince your opponent that he will lose. And make no mistake, there is a war going on, whether you want to admit it or not. It's very easy to lose a war that you refuse to acknowledge even exists. Engagement has failed, because Putin was never your friend. There is no common ground. Now he has revealed his true colors as a sworn enemy of the free world. And time is of the essence.

Thank you.

Mr. WICKER. Thank you very much, Mr. Kasparov.

Mr. Cotler.

IRWIN COTLER, PC, OC, CHAIR, RAOUL WALLENBERG CENTER FOR HUMAN RIGHTS

Mr. COTLER. Thank you, Senator. I'm delighted to be able to participate here in the common cause which brings us together, the struggle against the cultures of criminality and corruption and, in particular, the impunity that underpins them. And this is part of a large struggle for justice and accountability, both domestically and internationally. We meet, as has been mentioned, at an important moment of remembrance and reminder—the eighth anniversary of the torture and murder of Sergei Magnitsky, who not only uncovered the largest corporate tax fraud in Russian history, documented it, but paid for it with his life. And where, in a move that would make Kafka blush, Magnitsky was posthumously prosecuted for the very fraud and criminality that he had exposed.

The fifth anniversary of the adoption here in the United States of the Sergei Magnitsky Rule of Law Accountability Act and which, in particular, inspired other similar initiatives elsewhere, including in Canada, and the immediate aftermath of the unanimous adoption on October 18th by both houses of the Canadian Parliament of global justice for Sergei Magnitsky legislation, titled formally Justice for Victims of Corrupt Foreign Officials Act.

Accordingly, what I would like to do here is first summarize briefly the process in Canada as a matter of chronology and content that led to this historic, albeit belated, Canadian initiative; second, summarize the raison d'être for this legislation; and finally some brief comments dovetailing with what my colleagues and witnesses put forward to you—brief comments, where do we go from here in Canada and internationally.

First, having regard to the genesis and development of the Magnitsky process in Canada—it was inspired, not unlike the situation here in the U.S., by an encounter that I had with Bill Browder in 2010, and which led to the launch of the Justice for Sergei movement in Canada. A series of initiatives in November 2010 alone, following that encounter, provide a looking glass into the character and content of the movement, which included then a meeting of our foreign affairs subcommittee on international human rights, with Bill Browder as our principal witness on November 2nd, and then unanimous adoption by the foreign affairs subcommittee of my motion at the time calling inter alia for justice for Sergei Magnitsky legislation, modeled on the U.S. initiative.

One year later, I introduced a private members bill titled "An Act to condemn corruption and impunity in Russia in the case and death of Sergei Magnitsky," which was the first legislative initiative of its kind in the Canadian Parliament. But coming from an opposition party member, it required support from the government of the day, which regrettably was not forthcoming. In 2012, Boris Nemtsov, who has been mentioned, a leading Russian democrat, came to Canada to support my private member's bill, along with Vladimir Kara-Murza, and where he mentioned at the time, as has been characterized here, that justice for Sergei Magnitsky legislation would be the most pro-Russian legislation, on behalf of the Russian people, that we could adopt.

Later that year, together with Bill Browder and really under his leadership, we launched the Justice for Sergei Magnitsky Interparliamentary Group, which led to resolutions being adopted in the European Parliament, other European countries, and subsequently adoption of legislation itself in Estonia, Lithuania, and the like. In 2013, the pattern of unanimous motions continued, but the focus now shifted to making representations to the Canadian Government, where we conveyed the documentary evidence that you had collected here at the time, of 60 Russian officials. But our efforts, again, to get government action in Canada were unavailing.

The year 2014 began with Canada sanctioning Russian officials for their aggression in Crimea and Ukraine. And I remember saying at the time that had we moved earlier to sanction Putin's Russia for their domestic repression, we might have perhaps sent a signal that may have foreclosed the developing externalized aggression. And then Russia retaliated for those actions by banning 13

Canadian parliamentary leaders, including Member of Parliament Chrystia Freeland, who was later to become minister of foreign affairs, and myself, with respect to the Government [of Canada].

So I might add parenthetically that 12 of the 13 who were banned were all those who had taken a leadership role in the Canadian Parliament, in some level, in seeking sanctions for Russia's aggression in Crimea and Ukraine. I can say that I had not been as initiatory as they were, or as vocal as they were. So the Russians were asked, well, why did you ban Cotler? He wasn't as vocal anywhere as near as the other 12. And they said, oh, with Cotler, we have a long history. It goes back to 1979, when he was expelled for defending Russian dissidents. And the banning continued for another decade, et cetera. So Putin's Russia has a long memory, going back even to earlier times.

2015 witnessed a number of dramatic developments, which finally began to move us in the direction of legislation. In February 2015, Boris Nemtsov was murdered, right outside the Kremlin. This outrageous act provoked such a response in Canada, both within and without the Parliament, that in March 2015 the House unanimously adopted my motion calling for global justice for Sergei Magnitsky legislation—again, inspired by parallel developments here in the U.S. And I must say, in my remarks in the House at the time I said I could feel the spirit and inspiration of Boris Nemtsov when we unanimously adopted that motion.

In June, I introduced again a private member bill, this time global justice for Sergei Magnitsky legislation. The conservative government finally agreed to adopt this legislation. The process was adjourned, however, by the calling of an election in the summer of 2015. In the course of the election, all three parties committed themselves to adopt such legislation. The liberal party won the election, but the momentum for such legislation was stalled. References were made to the fact that we have sufficient existing sanctioning authority under our legislation, and that we didn't need a new legislation. That was the position of the then-Foreign Minister Stephane Dion. And that it might prejudice our, quote-unquote, "re-engagement" with Russia at the time.

Accordingly, we reignited the parliamentary process, now in both houses, and again with the witness testimony of Bill Browder, Vladimir Kara-Murza, Anna Nemtsova—Boris Nemtsov's daughter—and Garry Kasparov. A number of developing factors now underpinned that momentum, but I'll just mention two of them. A unanimous report from the foreign affairs committee calling for global justice for Sergei Magnitsky legislation. I have here the cover of the report[1] that came out of the parliamentary foreign affairs committee, as it had a picture of Sergei Magnitsky on the cover, to denote the legislation of Sergei Magnitsky's case and cause for the legislation.

As well——

Mr. WICKER. Sir, that is a report from the Canadian Parliament?

Mr. COTLER. Correct. Foreign affairs committee, unanimous report.

---

[1] The full report can be accessed at: http://www.ourcommons.ca/Content/Committee/421/FAAE/Reports/RP8852462/faaerp07/faaerp07-e.pdf

Mr. WICKER. Let's go ahead and put that in the record at this point. Without objection, that'll be done. You may proceed.

Mr. COTLER. I also might remark, the leadership of the newly appointed foreign minister Chrystia Freeland, who in May 2017 announced government support for Sergei Magnitsky legislation, following upon the report from the foreign affairs committee subsequent hearings as well. All of which led to a succession of Russian threats, emanating both from the Russian embassy in Canada and Putin himself, warning Canadian parliamentarians against adoption of what he called this toxic legislation, and the terrible impact it would have on Canada-Russia relations.

Fortunately, we had a Raoul Wallenberg all-party parliamentary caucus in Canada we initiated in 2016. And on the eve of the two houses voting on Sergei Magnitsky legislation, we called for not only the adoption of this legislation, but to make that adoption unanimous in both houses of parliament, so that we would send a message to Putin's Russia that we will not be intimidated and we will not be deterred by such threats. And so the legislation, and Bill Browder mentioned, was passed unanimously, 277 to zero, and received royal assent on the same day.

Let me now move to the second part of my comments, and very quickly, and that is the objectives and purposes of such legislation, the global justice for Sergei Magnitsky legislation in general, which you've now adopted here as well as that of the earlier justice for Sergei Magnitsky legislation.

First, to combat the persistent and pervasive culture of corruption, criminality, and impunity, and the externalized aggression abroad, of which Putin's Russia is a case study.

Second, to deter, thereby, other prospective violators, because if we indulge that culture of impunity in Russia or elsewhere, we only embolden the human rights violators. But if we sanction these violators, we can deter others because they know there's a price to be paid for their corruption and criminality.

Third, to make the pursuit of international justice a priority and a pillar of our human rights policy, both domestic and international. And I'm speaking both of the United States and Canada, and linking up with what Bill Browder said in that regard.

Fourth, to uphold the rule of law and justice and accountability in our own territories through the visa bans, asset seizures and the like. Recent evidence of how Magnitsky assets have been laundered in Canada is but one case study of the importance of having such comprehensive legislation.

Also, as it was argued yet again in the Russian threats that we are interfering with the sovereignty of Russia, our response has been: We are not interfering with the sovereignty of Russia or any other country. What we are seeking to do is to protect our own sovereignty, our own rule of law, our own economy, and exclude these would-be perpetrators from exercising what is, in effect, a privilege and not a right to enter our country.

Fifth, to protect Canadian businesses operating abroad. Magnitsky not only uncovered the largest corporate tax fraud in Russian history, but it was perpetrated against a U.K.-based entity, headed by Bill Browder, Hermitage Capital. So that this type of legislation would protect not only the integrity of commerce in Canada, but also our Canadian businessmen operating abroad.

Final point here: It's important to appreciate that this legislation targets human rights violators and not governments, targeting individuals and not governments themselves. Finally, and I think most importantly, it tells the human rights defenders, the Magnitskys of today, that they are not alone, that we stand in solidarity with them, that we will not relent in our pursuit of justice for them, and that we will undertake our international responsibilities in the pursuit of justice and the combatting of the cultures of criminality and corruption, let alone, in particular, the impunity.

And where do we go from here? Closing remarks. Number one, and I associate myself with all the initiatives that were suggested by Bill Browder in that regard. Third, and also connected with what he said, we need to internationalize the global justice for Sergei Magnitsky movement and secure as many participating countries as possible. As Boris Nemtsov put it: The adoption of Magnitsky legislation by EU countries would be a serious blow to the criminal regime in Russia. And as he added, if you want to protect yourself against Putin's thieves, murders, and corrupt officials—speaking to the European Parliament, you must adopt the Magnitsky law.

Fourth, as Bill put it, three of the G-7 countries have now adopted Magnitsky legislation. Canada assumes the presidency of the G-7. And the next G-7 meeting will be held in Quebec. We should seek to mobilize for such legislation in the four remaining G-7 countries, Germany, France, Italy, and Japan. And here, the United States has a distinguished and distinguishable role to play.

Five, we need to make the OSCE a focal point of our advocacy for justice for Sergei Magnitsky legislation, anchored in our commitments under the Helsinki Final Act. We have not only a right, but a responsibility to hold Russia, an OSCE State, accountable for its standing violations of its commitments under the Helsinki Final Act.

Sixth, the assault on human rights and the rule of law, and the imprisonment of human rights defenders in Russia, is a standing violation as well of Principle Seven of the Helsinki Final Act, the right of people to know and act upon their rights. And here, too, Russia must be accountable to free its political prisoners. Finally, from a global perspective, global justice for Sergei Magnitsky legislation can help us combat the resurgent global authoritarianism that we are witnessing today, and the culture of impunity that underpins it, by sanctioning human rights violators, be they in Russia, Venezuela, or South Sudan—which is something that Canada has done in the immediate aftermath of adopting our legislation—on October 18th we sanctioned 30 senior Russian violators, 19 Venezuelan officials including President Maduro, and three from South Sudan.

Mr. Chairman, we also—when I hear Bill Browder's testimony, need to reform the Interpol regime so that it is not used and abused in the way it has been. And our own minister of public safety, Ralph Goodale, in Canada, has announced that he is prepared to take the lead, in concert with others, for that purpose. At the end of the day, in adopting Magnitsky legislation, we make a statement not only of what we must do, but also of who we are.

Thank you, Mr. Chairman.

Mr. WICKER. Thank you very much. And thank you for your compelling testimony, to all three of you, and also for your courage. I know it's taken quite a bit.

Mr. Browder, just to follow up on that last point, there's no one in the leadership of Interpol that seriously is taking the position of the Russians, that you should be detained or arrested, is that correct? Is there a debate within Interpol?

Mr. BROWDER. Well, I'm not a member of Interpol. Russia is a member of Interpol. [Laughs.] And so they're accountable to their members, not to me, not to Irwin, not to Garry. And as such, as a member, they've been an errant member of Interpol. Interpol has rules that says they shouldn't be doing things like pursuing people for political purposes. And those rules have been upheld. Having said that, the Russians applied for me in 2013. Interpol rejected it.

They came back three weeks later. Russia applied, they rejected it again. They came back in 2014 and applied. Interpol rejected it again. And then, strangely, Interpol has allowed twice in this year, once just as I was coming to the United States to testify in front of the Senate Judiciary Committee and once right after the Canadian Magnitsky Act was passed, where they put me on the Interpol list, and I was on the Interpol list, accepted for some period of time.

And so there may be people in Interpol who are appropriately behaving. Having said that, Interpol is being abused wildly. And I'm not the only one. There are many other people who have suffered multiple attacks by Interpol where it's clearly been politically motivated. And so Interpol obviously needs to clean up their act if they're supposed to be a crime fighting organization, not a criminal organization, or an organization acting on behalf of criminals. And so there's serious reform that needs to be done.

Mr. WICKER. How transparent is the governing body of Interpol?

Mr. BROWDER. Interpol is a black box. Interpol is also very, unfortunately, unjudicially reviewable, which means that if somebody puts an arrest warrant out for you in any country, probably even North Korea, you have to go to a court—maybe not North Korea— but most countries you have to go to a court or the officials have to go to a court to get an arrest warrant. Interpol, there's no court. And you can't go to a court to appeal an Interpol red notice. So if they decide or they don't decide, there's no consequence. You can't sue them. You can't judicially review them. You can't do anything. And therefore, it continues to be a black box. The United States is probably the single largest contributor to Interpol. And the United States can fix Interpol, based on its financial contribution.

Mr. WICKER. I know others are anxious to ask questions. Let me give you an opportunity to clear up something. And I may have misspoken in my opening statement. Mr. Kasparov says follow the money. Mr. Cotler says something about laundering. How are you doing tracing the $230 million? And that really was stolen from the Russian people, was it not?

Mr. BROWDER. That's correct.

Mr. WICKER. OK, if you'd clear that up. Because I didn't want to imply that you, Bill Browder, lost $230 million. It was a fraudulent, ridiculous tax refund that raided the treasury that belonged to the Russian people. Would you comment on that?

Mr. BROWDER. That's a very important distinction. We did not lose any money in this fraud. The Russian people lost $230 million, which is what makes it so egregious. So——

Mr. WICKER. A very readily responded to request for a big refund on the Treasury.

Mr. BROWDER. On Christmas Eve 2007. The largest tax refund in Russian history. Granted without any questions asked.

Mr. WICKER. Right. Right. How we doing tracing where that money went?

Mr. BROWDER. Well, we've traced all the money. We found all the money. And the money has come to a lot of different countries. It's come to the United States. The Department of Justice froze $14 million that belonged to a company owned by the son of a Russian Government official called Prevezon. The money has gone to Switzerland. $20 million went to Switzerland. Prevezon's money and money belonging to the husband of the tax official who refunded it. Money went to the Netherlands. More than 3 million euros has been frozen by the Dutch authorities that belongs to Prevezon, again. Money went to France. About $8 million has been frozen in France. And there are criminal investigations now opened up in a dozen different countries. And I've learned a tremendous amount about money laundering in the last eight years, working with law enforcement, tracing this money, and helping law enforcement prosecute the people.

And this is where I become so agitated about the whole concept of cryptocurrencies and Bitcoin, because the reason we've been able to trace the $230 million is because when you send dollars or you send euros, in the dollars case, it goes through the Fed wire system. And there's a permanent trail of every movement of those dollars. And a permanent trail that goes back to banks and people and know your customer due diligence and authorities and regulators, et cetera. And that allows law enforcement and the good guys to get the bad guys, and stop the criminals. With Bitcoin and cryptocurrencies that's not possible. And two days ago one of Putin's economic advisors, Sergey Glazyev, publicly promoted the idea of cryptocurrencies to work around sanctions. And we really need to respond to this quickly.

We didn't respond to Facebook and Twitter quickly enough so that the Russians could do all sorts of crazy stuff in manipulating politics all over the world and that. Technology moved quicker than regulation. We're going to be in the exact same situation with cryptocurrencies unless we get on it very quickly.

Mr. WICKER. Thank you.

Mr. Cohen.

HON. STEVEN COHEN, COMMISSIONER, COMMISSION ON SECURITY AND COOPERATION IN EUROPE

Mr. COHEN. Thank you, Chairman.

I'm just in awe to be in front of you three gentlemen. This is probably as distinguished a panel as I've seen in my 11 years in

Congress. You've all had amazing lives, shown great courage, and changed the world for the better in a way that we all should be doing to advance freedoms and stand up for justice.

The Magnitsky law has obviously been effective, in that it is what has caused Mr. Putin and his government to take over and interfere with our elections. That is what they, I believe, see as a way to get the Magnitsky law repealed. They allegedly and apparently, and I believe, engaged in that meeting at Trump Tower for the purpose of getting relief on Magnitsky. It was not anything to do with adoption.

Do any of you have any information that you can give us concerning Russian involvement with our President, with our election processes, or with other information that we need to know? This is not a chess game. [Laughter.]

Mr. KASPAROV. First of all, I'd like just, Mr. Chairman, to make one comment, following Bill's words about Interpol. As a chairman of Human Rights Foundation, I've been dealing regularly with complaints from dissidents from many countries when authoritarian regimes have been abusing Interpol red notice to prosecute political leaders living in exile. This is a common practice. And it's not just only Russia. It's something inherently wrong with Interpol, which as Bill described is a black box. You can only see your name appearing or this red notice on internet, on a list, but you are not privy to any legal process, how they then appear there and what is in a notice sent by the government.

Unfortunately, quite a few authoritarian regimes are enjoying the rights to issue red notices. And if not for Bill's notoriety and his involvement in Magnitsky Act, he could be in real trouble. And thanks to the United States Senate and the House for defending him and removing him from the list. But many other people without the same prominence, they are just suffering. And there's very little can be done unless Interpol is faced with serious actions, starting here, to stop accommodating world dictators.

Now, regarding this involvement, there's certain things I can confirm from my own personal experience. For instance, I've no doubt, as someone who was raised in the Soviet Union and is familiar with the way the Communist system and KGB work, that this type of operation of meddling in the U.S. elections could be authorized only by Vladimir Putin. There's no way that it just could be done by some low-key operators. Clearly, the Magnitsky Act was one of the elements of this collusion and meddling. And the joke is that the word "adoption" now is used like a code name for sanctions and lifting sanctions.

And the Magnitsky law is viewed by Putin's regime as the core problem that started all other sanctions. So it's a top priority of Russian Government. And you could see the activities not only here, but across Europe to prevent other countries from entering the same legislation. And, again, while I cannot say anything with 100 percent confidence, but from my personal experience I believe that the Russian interference here had a clear goal of helping Putin regime out of the sanctions regime.

Mr. COHEN. Anybody else have anything to offer? Mr. Browder?

Mr. BROWDER. So, looking at this situation, Vladimir Putin, he runs a hundred operations with the expectation that 99 of them will fail. In terms of meddling with U.S. elections, meddling with British elections, meddling with Catalonian independence, meddling with German elections, meddling with French elections, it's a matter of fact that they do that. And the U.S. intelligence agencies have all confirmed that. The French intelligence agencies confirm that they were meddling in the French elections. It's now been confirmed that they were meddling in the Brexit debate.

And so there's no question about what Putin was doing. And the only question, which I don't have an answer to, is whether he was doing it on his own volition, or whether he was doing it in some type of agreement with the Trump administration. I have no evidence to argue one way or another on that second point, but I'm very satisfied that there is a credible law enforcement team put together that will answer that question, with 100 times the information that I have to be able to make that judgement.

Mr. COHEN. Thank you, sir.

Mr. Cotler——

Mr. WICKER. Thank you.

Ms. Moore.

Oh, Mr. Cotler, would you just respond.

Mr. COTLER. Yes, just very briefly, that in November, a Russian TV show featured Russian lawyer Natalia Veselnitskaya, with respect to the charges being brought against Bill Browder. This is the same person who, in a June 2016 meeting at Trump Tower in New York City with Donald Trump, Jr., at the time when it first came to light it appeared—and if you look at the news reports at the time—that all this was in relation to a Russian Government effort to aid Donald Trump's campaign by giving information that could be used against Hillary Clinton. However, it subsequently emerged that the real reason at the time was in order to bring about the repeal of the Magnitsky sanctions.

So one could see that even the interference in this American election had as its objective not only, if you will, matters relating to the election of Donald Trump against Hillary Clinton, but whoever was elected, to bring about the repeal of the Magnitsky sanctions. And in fact, right after President Putin was elected, back in 2012, his first foreign policy statement at the time addressed the issue of the odious Magnitsky sanctions.

So this is something that is top of mind and policy with regard to Putin's Russia, to the point where it's not only a case of interfering in elections, but it is also a brutal case of targeting the heroes of this movement. And in terms of not only the murder of Sergei Magnitsky, but Boris Nemtsov, who was the leading campaigner for justice for Sergei Magnitsky legislation internationally. And also, I believe, paid for it with his life. Vladimir Kara-Murza, who came before our foreign affairs subcommittee on human rights, testified, went back to Russia, was poisoned, almost died. Came back later after he had recovered, testified before our committee again, went back to Russia, was poisoned again and almost died.

You see the clear linkages here with regard to his testimony and then his poisoning. The death threats that have been received by my colleagues on this panel, the murder of witnesses related to subsequent proceedings regarding justice for Sergei Magnitsky legislation elsewhere, or lawyers connected with it. What you have here is a pattern of criminality and coverup that also must be seen in relation to the pattern of corruption and the pattern of interference in elections and the like.

Mr. COHEN. I have votes, so I have to leave. But I take my hat off to you. [Doffs hat.] And I would stay for the remainder of your testimony if I wouldn't be scolded by my leader.

Mr. WICKER. Well, Mr. Cohen, you tell them that they need to hold that vote open for Ms. Moore, because she's going to have an opportunity to ask her questions. So do what you can with the speaker.

Ms. Moore.

HON. GWEN MOORE, COMMISSIONER, COMMISSION ON SECURITY AND COOPERATION IN EUROPE

Ms. MOORE. Thank you so much, Senator Wicker.

And I just want to thank the panelists for being so brave. This is like something straight out of a spy novel. You can't make this stuff up.

I'm going to start out by asking a question—I'm embarrassed because I perhaps should know the answer to this. Mr. Browder, you say that there are 282 persons that should be on this Magnitsky list, and only 35 of them have been on the list, and that every December it's updated. Do we know yet if that list has been upgraded?

Mr. BROWDER. You shouldn't be embarrassed to ask the question, because I'm asking the same question myself. [Laughter.] So every year in December the list is added to. And every year in December it has been added to. We're now in December and it should be added to.

Ms. MOORE. Is this a U.S. Department of Justice's task?

Mr. BROWDER. This is the U.S. State Department and the U.S. Treasury Department. It will be published by the Treasury Department. It has been prepared together between the State and Treasury Department. They are the ones who have been delegated the responsibility to do this, and they're the ones who are supposed to do this. And I'm keeping my fingers crossed and hoping that they do do this, and that there's a very robust list that come out.

Ms. MOORE. Well, I think the Treasury Department has been a little busy lately. But having said that, do we know whether or not—this is the first year of a new administration, and a new Treasury Department and State Department. Have we had any indication in our communications—perhaps this is to Senator Wicker—that there's been an ability to compartmentalize enforcing the Magnitsky Act, and the President's disbelief, essentially, that the Russians interfered with our elections? Has there been any evidence that compartmentalization has happened—that we've been able to accomplish that?

Mr. BROWDER. We will only know——

Ms. MOORE. When the list comes out.

Mr. BROWDER. It's a very pregnant moment. Either the list will be published, or no list will be published—and each action will have a greater significance than just that list.

Ms. MOORE. I see. OK. Mr. Kasparov, you wrote a book, "Winter is Coming," and I guess you indicated that there's a new authoritarian playbook, and that previous totalitarian regimes have learned and upped their game. So can you just briefly share with us the evidence of those new tactics, what you think we ought to be able to do and perhaps what you think we can do about protecting the Voice of America and Radio Liberty.

Mr. KASPAROV. Just following your first question, I can add that from our observations this year the State Department was much less active than before. And maybe we'll see the sanctions list, but so far we don't have the same kind of activities that typically have been cooked within State Department, regarding Magnitsky law and other sanctions.

Now, speaking about new tactics, as a matter of fact, we saw it many years ago in Russia. And we have to give credit to Putin and his KGB cronies for changing the old-fashioned propaganda way of getting the story. Back in the Soviet days, they had a story to sell, the ideology. And it's always a problem because you have many arguments. Selling something requires power of conviction. And also, people may disagree. Putin's concept is different. It's not one story to sell, but it's basically telling you the truth is relative.

And they discovered this algorithm I think back in 2004–2005, when they realized that they had to deal with the growing influence of the internet in Russia. And there were two ways. One, you followed China and built a firewall. They didn't like it. and so they've moved into the sort of gray area, just using KGB tactics, creating some fake websites. They all presented some stories. Like, 90 percent of the true stories, but each site carried a piece that was part of the combined Kremlin message. They realized that if you have some websites that are allowed to criticize Putin and talking about corruption, these sites can defend KGB—telling that KBG involvement in apartment bombing in 1999 was a fake, and there's more credibility there.

By using these tactics in Russia, they saw this success and they moved to so-called near abroad, the former Soviet republics. Estonia was the first to be attacked. And then they moved to Europe. So when they actually entered the United States, this is the meddling in U.S. elections; they already had more than a decade of the experience of creating these fake websites, fake industry as an institution, the troll factories that have been in operation for more than a decade. And unfortunately, this country and the European Union paid more attention—or, actually, preferred to ignore the fact that Russia has been building its presence in media around the free world.

For instance, we look at the last elections in Germany. We have to give Putin credit for building Alternative for Germany, the Neo-Nazi party, almost from scratch by using Russian-German community and having the German-speaking media. And as a result, you have 94 Neo-Nazis in German Bundestag. So Putin just recognizes that the free world offered him many opportunities to play these games. And it's fairly cheap. You don't have to spend a lot of money for this good intervention. And unfortunately, it had worked.

Ms. MOORE. I thank you so much. And I sure feel anxious about the votes, but I just want to comment: We got about a half million sort of fake responses about net neutrality. It's a big deal with regard to whether or not the internet will have faster or slower lanes based on commercial interests. And they've been all tracked back to Russia. So this is a real threat at every level. I do thank you for your appearance. And I'm sorry that I have to leave so soon. But I leave you in very capable hands.

Mr. WICKER. Thank you, Ms. Moore.

And just in response, the State Department informs the Commission that the Magnitsky and Global Magnitsky lists will be published in the next week or two. So we'll see. And perhaps members of the State Department, staff members, are listening, even as we speak.

Senator Whitehouse.

HON. SHELDON WHITEHOUSE, COMMISSIONER, COMMISSION ON SECURITY AND COOPERATION IN EUROPE

Mr. WHITEHOUSE. Thank you. Thank you, Chairman.

And thank you to the panel for being here. You have all shown—indeed, exemplify—significant courage. And we are grateful to you.

I would like to propose to all of you the following thesis, and ask your reaction to it. The thesis has one broad element and a narrower element.

The broad element is that the true clash of civilizations in the world today is between the rule of law and countries that are governed by kleptocracy, autocracy, and criminality, that much of the evil that threatens our rule-of-law countries arises out of kleptocracy, autocracy, and criminality. And that consequentially it is a strategic imperative for the rule-of-law countries to address the underlying problem of kleptocrats, autocrats, and thieves. That's the broad part of the thesis.

The narrower part of the thesis is that the kleptocrats, tyrants and thieves ultimately seek sanctuary for their families, their assets, and themselves in rule-of-law countries. If you keep your ill-gotten gains in kleptocracy, autocratic, and corrupt countries, you're just waiting for the next bigger thief to come and steal what you have stolen. And the quality of life generally sucks. So they need to get out in order to succeed at their game. And here's where it gets a little bit smelly, because our laws, our lawyers, and other professionals provide and facilitate that very sanctuary. And the most prominent feature of that sanctuary is probably allowing shell and shelf corporations to obscure the identity of the kleptocrats, the autocrats, and the thieves so that law enforcement, the press, and others can't follow the connections.

I'll close my thesis by narrowing it right to this particular act, because it strikes me that shell and shelf corporations are a very useful device for the corrupt individuals specifically named in the Magnitsky Act to dodge around and find sanctuary for their assets, notwithstanding the law, by going through often sequential series of shell corporations so that ultimately it all turns up in the name of Wonderful Company, LLC someplace and, again, enjoying the protection of rule of law.

I'd love to have each of you react to that thesis at whatever level you choose.

Mr. Browder, you want to go first?

Mr. BROWDER. I could have given your speech just now. I agree with it 100 percent. The entire basis for the Magnitsky Act, inspiration for the Magnitsky Act, is exactly what you've just described, which is that these terrible people commit terrible crimes in their own countries. But they're so afraid that their money will be stolen, they want to keep it in countries that have a rule of law, that have property rights, and have institutions where they can be physically safe.

Mr. WHITEHOUSE. So the Magnitsky individuals, the ones identified in the law, are really the tip of a much, much bigger iceberg of kleptocracy and autocracy out there. And in the same manner that we have paid attention to these individuals, it would be wise for us as a nation to broaden our reach and more systematically address this problem of providing sanctuary for international evildoers.

Mr. BROWDER. Indeed. I would argue that we've come up with a good concept. But the devil is always in the details, and the devil is always within implementation. So as you've pointed out, people can obscure their ownership. They can do so with offshore companies, with nominees who don't even know they're nominees in offshore companies, and even in America, Canada, and various places like that. There are law firms, the enablers, who are actively assisting them, earning big fees with no consequences. And——

Mr. WHITEHOUSE. As a lawyer, let me point out that there are also accountants, realtors, yacht brokers, and various other professionals involved in these transactions as well. So, yes, the lawyers deserve some blame, but not all of it.

Mr. BROWDER. I don't want to single out the lawyers, but the lawyers have played a big role, no doubt.

Mr. WHITEHOUSE. They have played a big role and a nefarious one.

Mr. BROWDER. And I would actually say something that's quite controversial, and we've debated it here in the United States. We've debated it in Canada. We've debated it in the United Kingdom, as to what should be in the law. The law currently applies to the people who commit the crimes. If you really want to affect these people, you should include their family members. If somebody knows that not only will their freedoms be curtailed, but their family members will not be able to send their kids to Ivy League schools, to boarding schools in England. They won't be able to send their parents for medical treatment at Harley Street and at the Cleveland Clinic, all of a sudden, there's a totally different calculation. And that would actually seriously raise the effectiveness of this whole piece of legislation.

Mr. WHITEHOUSE. Mr. Kasparov.

Mr. KASPAROV. Yes, I couldn't agree more with your both broad and narrow thesis. Actually, we're talking about a system. It's $230 million is the tip of the iceberg, maybe it's a drop in the sea, because thanks to Bill Browder, and his efforts, you know, you could discover every penny of this 230 million [dollars]. But we were probably talking about an amount close to $1 trillion that has been spread around. So using similar schemes of looting money in Russia and parking them, not in China, not in Venezuela, not in Iran, but in this country, in the United Kingdom, in France, and you name it—in countries where, as you said, this money is protected by the rule of law.

And Putin realized that the Magnitsky law was an imminent threat to the very foundation of his power, which was based on a guarantee for all members of the gang to loot Russia, to steal money there, and to place it safely anywhere in the world they choose. And by the mafia rule, you have to offer full protection to the last hitman in exchange for absolute loyalty. That's why when I heard the comments from some of the opponents of Magnitsky law saying, "Oh, they are just, you know, second or third tier of officials, why should we pay attention?"

It's about principle. Because the moment that one person is not protected anymore stealing money in Russia, and having them also protected in the United States or in Europe, on the rule of law, the whole system will collapse. And that's why Putin was so eager, and is spending massive resources, to repeal Magnitsky law and prevent countries, like with open threats to Canadian Parliament, just it's unheard. The way the Russian Parliament and Putin himself actively trying to stop Canadians blackballing them with all sorts of retaliations.

And as you said, it's the modern autocrats are working, because they want to enjoy the luxuries of the world that they are fighting with, for propaganda purposes. And that's why they're far more vulnerable than the Communist regime. And I've been saying for a long time, use not tanks but banks. And they found a way of corrupting Western financial, political, and business circles, by doing it for years. And we have to give Putin credit for just being quite savvy in just finding the soft spots.

And finally, I could say that for those who have been arguing about his openness, saying, oh, if we have this engagement it will help to sort of lift Russian standards to the world's accepted rules and laws and regulations. Actually, it works the other way around. It's not that Russia upgraded its rules and regulations, but it corrupted the free world that was absolutely open and defenseless against the flood of these hundreds of billions of dollars of money stolen in Russia. And I believe the system has been in place for many other authoritarian regimes that followed Putin's model.

Mr. WHITEHOUSE. Mr. Cotler, final thoughts to add?

Mr. COTLER. Yes, Senator. I appreciate your characterization of the clash of civilizations in terms of the rule of law, and the autocracy, kleptocracy, and criminality, and that it's a strategic imperative at this point to combat them. I want to say that I think this is being enhanced, both the threat and the imperative; by this resurgent global authoritarianism; by the illiberal populism; and by something we haven't spoken of, but I think is becoming particularly worrisome, and that's of democracies in retreat or the idea of democracy, the institutions of democracy being increasingly questioned even in democratic countries, aided and augmented by the post-truth universe.

And so I just want to bring to your attention something that I think you know but maybe should be part of our overall internationalization of advocacy, and that is, recently in Prague, in October—under the auspices of Prague 2000, which are sort of the heirs of Vaclav Havel's intellectual and moral initiatives—Europeans and Americans and others gathered together to launch the Prague Declaration [sic; Appeal] for Democratic Renewal, and this

Prague declaration seeks to address, in a way, what you have been speaking of, Senator, and seeks to mobilize democracies, at this point, in a coalition for democratic renewal in order to reaffirm the values, the ideas, the institutions of democracy in democratic countries. And I think this is something that we may be able to factor into our work here with regard to the Helsinki Final Act, Justice for Sergei Magnitsky case and cause and the like.

Mr. WHITEHOUSE. Well, thank you for your leadership.

I've taken a lot of time, Mr. Chairman. Let me just, in closing, thank not only you and the Helsinki Commission for the work that is being done in this area, but I want to recognize the Center for Strategic and International Studies and the Kremlin Playbook document that they put together under the leadership of Heather Conley. I want to recognize the Atlantic Council's work and the Kremlin Trojan Horse document that they put together. I want to recognize the Hudson Institute, whose Kleptocracy Initiative is doing powerful work in this area. So there are a number of important voices that are joining together, and I hope we can take advantage of that broad support to continue to take action against the imperiling cabal of kleptocracy, autocracy, and crime that is a strategic threat to our country.

Thank you, Chairman.

Mr. WICKER. Thank you for that very valuable line of questioning, Senator Whitehouse, and let me just follow up—and it may be that Senator Whitehouse is aware of this or not—there's a man named Paul Ostling, a former COO of Ernst & Young, who blew the whistle on a company in Russia that had powerful friends in the Kremlin. The Russians are now using the American legal system to commence litigation against Mr. Ostling, a process which has substantially depleted his own fortunes.

I don't know if any of you are familiar with this, but I am convinced that that is actually happening. So this would be a case in which American law firms are being hired by Russians to harass people who legitimately came forward and blew the whistle, much as you did, Mr. Browder, and much as Sergei Magnitsky did.

Are any of you aware of this, and is this happening writ large, or was it only to an isolated few like Mr. Ostling?

Mr. BROWDER. I haven't heard the story, but I just wrote down his name so I can do some research, but more generally, Putin interferes using our freedom of the press, he interferes using democracy, he interferes using the internet, and he also interferes abusing legal processes—we've talked about Interpol and so on—but they also interfere very aggressively using American law firms.

And Senator Whitehouse, no offense to lawyers, but there are a lot of sleazy lawyers who are actively making huge amounts of money—American lawyers ripping human rights activists and others limb from limb using the American legal process. And I've been on the other side of this where I had a lawyer who worked for me helping to track down the stolen money from the Magnitsky crime. His name was John Moscow, a former prosecutor from BakerHostetler law firm, and we then found the money, presented it to the Department of Justice, and he switched sides and then started from representing the victims to representing the perpetrators to make tens of millions of dollars. He was disqualified by the

Second Circuit after a year and half, but he was ready to basically throw out his entire integrity as a lawyer to work for the Russian Government to terrorize a whistleblower that he helped. So there's a lot of bad guys out there doing this stuff. I'm going to look into Mr. Ostling because I think that sounds like an important story.

Mr. WICKER. Mr. Cotler, are the signatories to the Prague declaration current members of the government or former members of the governing majority?

Mr. COTLER. The signatories to the Prague declaration include both present and former parliamentarians——

Mr. WICKER. So it's bipartisan.

Mr. COTLER. It's utterly bipartisan. I might add that the National Endowment for Democracy here, under the leadership of Carl Gershman, was very much engaged in the drafting of the Prague declaration, and you've got congresspeople, senators, Canadian parliamentarians, Europeans, artists, intellectuals, et cetera. It's an attempt to mobilize a movement of an international character for the renewal of democracy and for the revival of the import and impact of the democratic idea.

Mr. WICKER. Thank you.

Mr. Kasparov, Natan Sharansky once said, a country that does not respect the rights of its own people will not respect the rights of its neighbors. And, in essence, we're all neighbors in this global economy we have.

So I would ask you, in that regard, what's it to somebody in Providence, Rhode Island, or Tupelo, Mississippi, or Milwaukee, Wisconsin, that we're so interested in this Magnitsky List? Why should someone in Memphis approve of us shining the light of day on this issue? What's their stake in this?

Mr. KASPAROV. By the way, I'm one of the signatories of Prague's declaration, so—[laughs]—that was mentioned.

Mr. WICKER. I think it enhances the declaration.

Mr. KASPAROV. Yes, yes. It goes back to my statement—and I've been saying it for many years, and Boris Nemtsov and many others repeated it as well—that Putin was our problem but eventually it would be everybody's problem. And Putin has no other choice but to create chaos, spread chaos. Russian economy is not in good shape, and he doesn't believe it will ever offer him an excuse for staying in power indefinitely.

So if you listen to Russian talk shows, you will not hear anything about Russia. It's all about Ukraine, Syria, of course United States. It is 24/7 anti-American bashing because America is enemy that Putin wants to oppose, even virtually, to show his strengths, to expose the aura of invincibility. And, for him, meddling in American election was just part of the game. He will never stop doing that because he has nothing else to offer to people in Russia.

His domestic propaganda is filled with his geopolitical adventures, and if you think that he will leave you alone, no, because he has to prove every day that he is invincible. That's the rule of the mafia. The moment he looks weak, he will be challenged, and Putin instinctively knows this rule, so he cannot project any weakness, and the best way to pretend he is strong is to defy the biggest power in the world.

And these latest interferences just demonstrate it—not only in America, in Europe as well—that he would do it, and he will always look for soft spots. He is a great opportunist. He saw opportunity in Syria, he went on, and he just carpet-bombed Aleppo, pushing refugees in Europe to create political crisis there and help alt-right that always wanted to leave sanctions. So he's looking at this big map as an opportunity to spread chaos.

And for those who think that you can find common ground with him, you're wrong. And Putin, he's at a point where he will be looking for more conflicts, and because he is the KGB guy and also Judo expert, he looks for an opportunity to use the strengths of the free world against the free world itself, so that's why he looks for the pillars of the free world, like innovations, technology, rule of law, as an element of his hybrid war against the free world, which gives him a purpose of staying in power forever.

Mr. WICKER. I think the people who would like to have avoided this kleptocracy and all of the bad things in Senator Whitehouse's thesis, I think we missed a real opportunity in the early 1980s. That's my conclusion.

Give us some hope, Mr. Kasparov—and I'll let you go first, and then others, also. Is there a generation out there waiting inside Russia to do right by the Russian people? Give us some hope that we're headed somewhere to a better place. I realize you are only 32 years old.

Mr. KASPAROV. I'm an acute optimist by nature, though I have to live in exile for almost five years. From history books I know that every dictatorship comes to an end, and the Putin-like dictatorship is very vulnerable to geopolitical defeat. I could remind people about the orderly retreat of Soviet troops from Afghanistan in 1989. It was nothing like American stampede in Saigon, but the very picture of Russian troops retreating—Soviet troops—in February 1989 sent a very powerful signal to Eastern Europe and to the former Soviet republics that empire are no longer all powerful, it's weakening. And by the end of the year, the Soviet Empire in Eastern Europe collapsed; in less than three years after the retreat from Afghanistan, the Soviet Union ceased to exist.

I think that what we saw in the last year, thanks to Alexei Navalny and his efforts of bringing young people to the streets, there's a generation that is not happy, but nobody will challenge dictator and dictatorship if it looks strong. You need just to create image of weaknesses, and the moment it happens, I believe the change could be all of a sudden.

I've no idea how and when Putin's regime will collapse, and that's bad news. The good news: Putin also doesn't know it as well.

Mr. WICKER. Mr. Whitehouse, I think what I'd like to do is give each member of the panel, starting with Mr. Cotler, an opportunity to take a moment or two and summarize. But before that, if you have other questions, I'd recognize you for another round.

Mr. WHITEHOUSE. No, thank you. I'd be delighted to hear the closing statements.

The only thing that I would do is take advantage of your generosity to read two sentences from our own Helsinki Commission report, "Corruption in Russia: An Overview." One says: "To avoid sanctions, Putin's cronies take advantage of the secrecy provided by

Western offshore havens to secure stolen funds abroad." That is what we are talking about, and clearly, one of the offshore havens—in fact, unfortunately a growing offshore haven—is our own country now.

And second: "Any anti-corruption measures implemented in the West undermine Putin's kleptocracy." End quote. So not only are we, to some degree, sowing the seeds of our own destruction by providing secrecy for these international criminals, but we very much have it within our power to unwind that by taking anti-corruption measures, to quote our own report, "implemented in the West."

So I applaud the work that the Helsinki Commission staff have done on that report. I wanted to highlight those particular points. I thank you for this hearing, and I am eager to hear the closing remarks of our witnesses.

Mr. WICKER. Let's just ask Mr. Cotler to take a moment or two and make any points that haven't been made, or respond to anything that needs to be nailed down.

Mr. COTLER. Well, Mr. Chairman, I might just respond to your words in terms of the Russian generation today. I think that they are legatees of great leaders, of whom Andrei Sakharov was the father of the modern dissident movement, and his words, as he put it, "I do not know what will help the cause of human rights. I do know that it will not be helped by silence." Just as Elie Wiesel, great Nobel Peace laureate, said that the real danger is silence in the face of evil, and that it's our responsibility, wherever we are, to speak out and act against injustice. And that's what the Helsinki Final Act was intended to do, that's what Justice for Sergei Magnitsky legislation was intended to do.

And your remarks with regard to Sharansky—I happen to have had the great fortune to have acted as counsel for Anatoly Sharansky when he was in the Soviet Union. We'd become very close friends. But I think his own voyage is very interesting in terms of an inspirational voyage.

Sharansky was one of the three founders of the Helsinki monitoring groups in the former Soviet Union. It was those monitoring groups, founded under the Helsinki Final Act—the right to know and act upon one's rights—that helped bring about, if I can use a Marxist metaphor, the withering away of the former Soviet Union. They demonstrated how a few small people can transform the world. I think that sends a message to young people in Russia, but also to people here in the United States and Canada, wherever they may be, that acting together in concert on behalf of a just cause can, in fact, change the world.

And I will close by saying that Vladimir Kara-Murza, when he testified before us and said that he believes that the younger generation in Russia will demonstrate that, if given the support of the international community in terms of combatting the cultures of criminality and corruption and impunity so that they can give expression to their ideals, they, too, can do what the Sharanskys did and change the universe. And it may be that Putin's Russia, in not too long, will also wither away as did previous totalitarian regimes. But we have to play our part in seriously and internationally combatting this resurgent global authoritarianism and the cultures of criminality, corruption and, in particular, the impunity that underpins it.

Mr. WICKER. Mr. Kasparov.

Mr. KASPAROV. Very quickly—so I think that Magnitsky's Act gives this country and American allies around the world a unique opportunity to demonstrate its support for Russian people, to make a clear distinction between the criminal regime that is running Russia today, and looting Russian resources, and parking money in the world under the pretext of rule of law. It brings back the memories of very strong language used by Ronald Reagan condemning communist crimes, but always emphasizing that it's not about the people of the Soviet Union, who were also victims of totalitarian regime.

I think just making this clear distinction and also sending a message that the money, this loot that is being parked in the free world, will be eventually returned to Russia to help Russian people to rebuild the country after the collapse of Putin's criminal enterprise. That will be very important, and hopefully it will change the mood, if not of all Russians, but many young people that will recognize that America and the free world is not fighting Russia, as Putin is trying to pretend, but fighting the criminals who are hurting Russia as much as the rest of the world.

Mr. WICKER. Thank you.

Mr. Browder.

Mr. BROWDER. So why is Putin so mad at this? Why is he mad at me? Why is he mad at you? Why is he mad at this concept of Magnitsky Act, Magnitsky sanctions? He's mad because, although Washington is not the center of innovation and technology, you and your colleagues have come up with a new technology for dealing with human rights abuse here in Washington. You've been the big innovators. And you found the Achilles' heel of the Putin regime.

As Garry has said, as Vladimir Kara-Murza has said, as Boris Nemtsov has said—the Soviet Politburo didn't go on vacation to St. Tropez and South Beach, but the people from the Putin regime do, and we figured out their Achilles' heel, and we know it. And we should use it, and we should use it aggressively, and we should use it going forward, and we shouldn't be shy about using it.

Thank you for doing this today.

Mr. WICKER. And thanks to all three members of the panel and to the members of the Commission who were here today, and this hearing is now closed.

[Whereupon, at 11:23 a.m., the hearing ended.]

APPENDICES

PREPARED STATEMENTS

PREPARED STATEMENT OF HON. ROGER WICKER, CHAIRMAN,
COMMISSION ON SECURITY AND COOPERATION IN EUROPE

The Commission will come to order. Good morning. Welcome to today's hearing on "The Magnitsky Act at Five Years: Assessing Accomplishments and Challenges."

Before we begin today, I want to recognize Ambassador David Killion, the Helsinki Commission Chief of Staff, who is retiring at the end of this month after 23 years of Federal Service. Senator Cardin and I joined together to appoint Ambassador Killion to direct the Commission at a key moment—shortly after Russia's invasion of Crimea in 2014.

Since then, Ambassador Killion's leadership has contributed greatly to enhancing the stature and the impact of our Commission as it develops U.S. policy responses to critical security threats in the OSCE region. With his considerable diplomatic skills, he has also managed to keep our Commission unified, enabling us to speak with a strong voice when necessary on issues such as Russia's violation of its Helsinki commitments. In addition, Ambassador Killion has extended Commission leadership to new and critically relevant policy areas, such as the effort to combat kleptocracy. As such, this hearing is a perfect capstone to Ambassador Killion's work for us. Ambassador, thank you for your public service.

This is the Commission's final hearing in 2017, and I cannot think of a more fitting way to end the year than to revisit one of the signature pieces of legislation that has come out of the Helsinki Commission.

The Magnitsky Act was drafted to hold accountable the Russians who were responsible for the torture and murder of tax attorney Sergei Magnitsky in 2012. Why was the Helsinki Commission concerned with this particular crime?

The mandate of the Helsinki Commission requires us to "monitor the acts of the signatories which reflect compliance with or violation of the articles of the Final Act of the Conference on Security and Cooperation in Europe," also known as the Helsinki Final Act. Those articles deal with commitments in three major areas, or "baskets"—security, economics, and the human dimension.

The case that ended with Sergei Magnitsky's tragic death concerned major violations in two of those three "baskets"—massive corruption in Russia, which the OSCE attempts to deal with through economic measures, and the egregious human rights violations involved in the unspeakable treatment of Sergei Magnitsky.

(33)

The five years that have elapsed since the passage of the Magnitsky Act—and the eight years that have elapsed since Sergei Magnitsky's murder—have certainly shown that our concern with Russia's unchecked corruption and wanton disregard for human rights was well founded. In that time corruption has continued to eat away at the fabric of Russian society, enabling further misbehavior both within and beyond Russia's borders. The state at this point can truly be described as a kleptocracy, where Putin rules with the help of a group of cronies whose loyalty is guaranteed by transfers of wealth stolen from the Russian people.

Russia has violated the territorial integrity of a European State and interfered in the elections of a number of OSCE participating states, including the United States. And, of course, Russian citizens continue to suffer from the predations of their own government on a daily basis. Russian opposition politician Boris Nemtsov, who was himself murdered in 2015 within sight of the Kremlin walls, deemed the Magnitsky Act "the most 'pro- Russia' law—for justice." We do sincerely hope that the Magnitsky Act will one day lead to justice—not only for Sergei Magnitsky and his family and friends, but also for all Russians who suffer violations of their universal rights by a state that believes it is accountable to no one.

We have three remarkable witnesses to speak to us today about what the Magnitsky Act has accomplished, as well as what still needs to be done to encourage Russia to respect the rights of its citizens and live up to its OSCE commitments.

We will hear first from William Browder, the CEO of Hermitage Capital, the firm that was plundered to the tune of $230 million in a massive tax evasion scheme by Russian authorities. Mr. Browder has worked tirelessly for the past eight years, at great risk to his own safety, to bring those responsible for Sergei Magnitsky's murder to justice. I strongly encourage any of you who have not read his book "Red Notice" to pick up a copy and do so. It is a gripping and unforgettable account of massive corruption, torture, murder, and impunity.

After that, Garry Kasparov will provide us with a broader view, addressing the full scope of corruption and human rights violations in Russia. Mr. Kasparov is well known to most of us as one of the greatest chess players in history, becoming the youngest world champion ever at age 22 in 1985. After 20 years at the top of the chess world, he gave it up and joined the fledgling Russian pro-democracy movement in 2005. He participated, along with Boris Nemtsov, in the May 2012 Bolotnaya Square demonstrations, one of the biggest protests held in Russia since the 1990s. The Bolotnaya Square protests were followed by an extensive crackdown that forced him to leave the country and relocate to New York. Mr. Kasparov is the chairman of the New York-based Human Rights Foundation, and he has also found the time to write a book entitled "Winter Is Coming: Why Putin and the Enemies of the Free World Must Be Stopped." Although I have not had an opportunity to read the book in its entirety, I certainly agree with its premise: The free world needs to stand up to the threat that Russia poses to core Helsinki Act principles. I believe this is the first time we have ever had a world chess champion testify at a Helsinki

Commission hearing, and we are very much looking forward to hearing what Mr. Kasparov has to say.

Finally, the Honorable Professor Irwin Cotler will testify about his work to pass a Canadian version of the Magnitsky Act. The pressure from Russia on Mr. Cotler and other Canadian backers of that bill has been immense—just as it has been in every other country that has considered passing a version of the Magnitsky Act. Professor Cotler has a distinguished career in advancing human rights around the world, not only as Canada's Attorney General and Justice Minister, but also as the founder and chair of the Raoul Wallenberg Center, an institution dedicated to bringing together all parts of civil society in the defense of human rights. We welcome your thoughts on what the international community should do to address the scourge of Russian corruption and impunity.

Again, we thank you for being here, and thank you for your full written statements, which will be included in the record.

PREPARED STATEMENT OF HON. CHRIS SMITH, CO-CHAIRMAN,
COMMISSION ON SECURITY AND COOPERATION IN EUROPE

Mr. Chairman, I would like to take the opportunity to thank our distinguished guests for being with us today and marking the fifth anniversary of the Sergei Magnitsky Rule of Law Accountability Act.

This all began with Sergei's investigation into the brazen theft of $230 million from the Russian people by officers of FSB Unit K and the Interior Ministry. He continued to expose Colonel Artem Kuznetsov and Major Pavel Karpov's plunder from foreign investors and how they lavishly spent it, while millions of Russians struggled to get by. For that, Kuznetsov and Karpov illegally detained Sergei, repeatedly tortured him, and denied him medical attention. All in the hope that they could force Sergei to confess and absolve themselves of their crimes. Sergei was murdered because he would never confess to trumped up charges, and never gave into to Kuznetsov and Karpov's brutality.

The Senate and the House passed the Sergei Magnitsky Act five years ago to ensure that Sergei and his family got the justice they deserved and to send a message to Russia: "This shall not stand." The identification and sanction of those involved in all aspects of Sergei's illegal detention, torture, and murder struck right at the heart of the Kremlin elite. It sent an unmistakable signal that the United States of America is prepared to sanction all those involved in human rights abuses.

In response, President Putin took his wrath out on innocent Russian orphans. These children, many of whom were in need of serious medical attention, had their hopes of a loving family and a happier life dashed—dashed because the Kremlin elite saw harming vulnerable children as the best means to retaliate against the United States. Nineteen children died who could have been helped, had they been adopted and brought to the U.S.

Furthermore, Putin, still reeling from the impact of the Magnitsky Act, lashed out at the United States, and those he saw as responsible for the law, including myself and others in this room. Despite having traveled to Russia many times, I was denied a Russian visa in 2013. I had planned a trip to discuss the impact of the Magnitsky Act inside Russia, but my application was ignored. The Russian Ambassador gave no explanation for my denial, but I think we all know why it happened. Russia saw me as a threat, because the Sergei Magnitsky Act had hurt them.

More than 40 years on from the signing of the Helsinki Final Acts, the human rights situation in Russia continues to deteriorate. But the Magnitsky Act wounded President Putin and his close circle. It took away that which was most dear to the Kremlin elite—their freedom to travel to the U.S. and to safeguard their money in our nation. The law set the standard around the world for other legislation that would freeze the assets and travel of Russian human rights abusers.

I would once again like to thank the witnesses for attending this hearing, and their dedication to exposing the malicious and insidious nature of President Putin's regime. Mr. Chairman, I yield my time.

PREPARED STATEMENT OF WILLIAM BROWDER, CEO, HERMITAGE
CAPITAL MANAGEMENT

Chairman Wicker, Ranking Member Cardin, distinguished members of the Commission, thank you for the opportunity to share my views on the Magnitsky Act today.

When my lawyer, Sergei Magnitsky, was murdered on November 16, 2009, after uncovering massive state corruption in Russia, it was the most heart-breaking moment of my life. Sergei had been killed because he was my lawyer. He would still be alive today if he hadn't worked for me.

As I began the fight for justice for Sergei, I encountered all sorts of opposition in Russia and abroad. I could never have imagined that day when I learned of his murder that there would someday be a U.S. human rights law bearing his name. But five years ago today, on December 14, 2012, the President of the United States signed the Sergei Magnitsky Rule of Law Accountability Act into law.

Moreover, on the day it passed, I could never have predicted how far the Magnitsky Act would spread around the world. Without exaggeration, it has become the most important piece of human rights legislation passed in this century.

As I sit in front of you today, I want to underline that the entire Magnitsky movement started right here at the Helsinki Commission nine years ago.

In April, 2009, when Sergei Magnitsky was still alive, I met Kyle Parker, a staff member at the Commission. I briefed him on how Sergei had been falsely arrested and imprisoned in retaliation for uncovering and exposing a $230 million tax rebate fraud committed by officials of the Russian state. Upon hearing the story, Mr. Parker recommended that I present Sergei's case at a full Commission hearing in the summer of 2009. It was at that point that Senator Cardin became aware of Sergei's story.

When Sergei was murdered on November 16, 2009, Senator Cardin immediately took it upon himself to see that this terrible injustice would not go without consequences. He worked with Senators Wicker, McCain and Lieberman as well as the Helsinki Commission staff, and together they introduced the Magnitsky Act in October, 2010. Representative McGovern led the parallel effort in the House of Representatives.

They did so at a moment when the U.S. government's policy was to reset relations with Russia. At the time, the U.S. Administration was firmly against antagonizing the Russian government in any way, and based on the public feedback of the Russian government, the Magnitsky Act would do just that.

Even though it appeared that the bill had little chance of passage due to the president's opposition, I was overwhelmed and touched to see so many Russian activists like the late Boris Nemtsov, Ludmila Alexeeva and Garry Kasparov take up Sergei's cause and publicly call for a Magnitsky Act to be adopted. Having this public discourse was a small measure of justice in and of itself.

It turned out that everyone's pessimism was misplaced. The nearly biblical nature of Sergei's sacrifice took on a life of its own and created a rare moment where morality would overcome the cold calculations of realpolitik.

The bill came up for vote in Congress in November, 2012, winning overwhelming bi-partisan support. It passed the House 365–43 and the Senate 92–4. It was signed into law by President Obama on December 14, 2012.

The power of the Magnitsky Act did not stop there. Senators Cardin, Wicker and McCain realized that they had stumbled onto a new technology for dealing with human rights abuse. In the past, murderous dictatorships like the Khmer Rouge didn't go on vacation to St. Tropez and South Beach, but in today's globalized world these kinds of dictators do. The Senators asked, "Why shouldn't the Magnitsky Act be applied globally?" and in 2015 launched the Global Magnitsky Act.

Because the bill continued the Magnitsky legacy, the Kremlin was dead set against it. In the spring and summer of 2016, the Kremlin-linked lawyer, Natalia Veselnitskaya, worked with a team of expensive DC lobbyists, PR firms, private investigators and other operatives, sparing no expense to try to stop the Global Magnitsky Act or to have Sergei's name removed from it. Thankfully, these efforts were not successful.

After the bill passed with a similar overwhelming majority in both Houses of Congress, the president signed the Global Magnitsky Act into law on December 23, 2016.

After this, the dominoes began to fall around the world. In December, 2016, the Estonian Parliament passed the Estonian Magnitsky Act by a unanimous vote of 90–0. In May, 2017, the British Parliament passed their equivalent to the Magnitsky Act into law, allowing the British government to seize assets of human rights violators. In October, 2017, the Canadian Parliament voted 277–0 in favor of a Canadian Magnitsky Act. Then, on November 16, 2017—the eighth anniversary of Sergei's murder—the Lithuanian Parliament passed their Magnitsky Act 71–0.

Parliaments in Ukraine, South Africa and Gibraltar are each drafting their own Magnitsky Acts and will be considering them in the near future. We're working with parliamentarians in other countries to introduce similar Magnitsky legislation.

All of this started here. I could never have imagined that a single hearing at the Helsinki Commission would have turned into this historic global justice movement.

Critics of the Magnitsky Act claim that all it does is antagonize Vladimir Putin and is not effective. However, the evidence points to the contrary.

When Mikhail Khodorkovsky, the oligarch who crossed Putin and who was imprisoned for nearly ten years, was released in 2014, he told me that after the Magnitsky Act passed there was a noticeable improvement in the treatment of prisoners. The guards were all terrified of being added to the Magnitsky list themselves.

Russian judges are equally scared of being added to the Magnitsky list. Not a month goes by without a headline from the Russian courts where Sergei Magnitsky's name is mentioned as other victims highlight their own abuse.

Most importantly, we know how effective the Magnitsky Act is because of Putin's own reaction. In 2012, he publicly stated that repealing Magnitsky-like sanctions was one of his single largest foreign policy priorities. This led to a whole series of efforts culminating in the now notorious meeting between Natalia Veselnitskaya and Trump representatives at Trump Tower. This exhaustive campaign underlines just how high a priority this is for Putin.

For me, Putin's desire to discredit the Magnitsky Act came at a high personal cost.

In July, 2013, shortly after the Magnitsky Act was passed, Putin put me on trial *in absentia* for trumped-up tax charges along with Sergei Magnitsky, three years after Sergei's murder. Sergei was the first person to be tried posthumously in Russian history. We were both found guilty and I was sentenced to nine years in a Russian prison colony.

Even before this verdict, the Russian government applied to Interpol for a Red Notice for my arrest. They also applied to the British authorities to have me extradited from the U.K. Both of those requests were refused because they were deemed to be illegitimate and politically motivated.

But that didn't stop Putin. He was so angry that, in spite of the previous rejection, his government re-applied to Interpol four more times. The most recent Interpol request from Russia came on the same day that the Magnitsky Act was signed into law in Canada in October, 2017. This request and all others have been rejected. In fact, after this last rejection, Interpol has sent a notice to all member states instructing them not to cooperate with Russia on any further attempts to have me arrested.

Putin was no more effective in his attempts with the British government. The Kremlin applied to U.K. law enforcement agencies a dozen different times for mutual legal assistance and my extradition. All of these requests have been firmly rejected by the British government.

Even though Putin fails every time, he hasn't given up. When the bogus tax-evasion charges went nowhere, he decided to escalate with even more ridiculous allegations against me. The Russian government accused me of stealing $4.8 billion of IMF funds destined for Russia during the 1998 currency collapse; they accused me of being an MI6 and CIA dual agent intent on destabilizing Russia; they accused me of being a serial killer, responsible for the murder of Russian criminals who were involved in the $230 million tax rebate fraud; and finally they even accused me of killing Sergei Magnitsky himself.

Putin's rage was not confined to absurd criminal accusations. He's taken more traditional criminal approaches as well. Kremlin agents have made multiple death threats against me. The most serious of which came from Dmitry Medvedev, the Russian prime minister, who told a gathering of journalists at the World Economic Forum in Davos in 2013 that, "It's a shame that Sergei Magnitsky is dead and Bill Browder is alive and running around." In the summer of 2015, I received a message from a senior U.S. official that the U.S. government was aware of efforts to organize a rendition plot to illegally kidnap me and bring me back to Russia.

Why is Putin so invested in this? Because this goes to the core of his kleptocratic regime. Unlike in Soviet times, today the Kremlin does not commit crimes for ideological reasons. They commit crimes for money. In this case, the theft of $230 million. Over the last eight years we've investigated who got that money and found that Putin himself was a recipient of proceeds of this crime through his closest childhood friend, Sergei Roldugin, a famous cellist.

We have also discovered that the head of the Russian tax office, Olga Stepanova, who authorised the illegal tax refund, as well as two other tax officials, Olga Tsareva and Elena Anisimova, also received proceeds from the crime.

In 2013, the U.S. Department of Justice discovered that a company owned by Denis Katsyv, the son of the former vice-chair of the Moscow region, where some of the cover-up of the crime took place, was also a recipient.

This summer we discovered that a Russian/Syrian national named Issa al-Zeydi received millions from the fraud on a corporate account in Cyprus. Issa al-Zeydi was named by the U.S. Treasury as a person providing material support for the Assad regime.

At present, a dozen countries have launched criminal investigations into the recipients and launderers of the stolen $230 million that Sergei Magnitsky uncovered. We expect more individuals and companies will be exposed and charged in the future.

Putin's reaction has been so extreme because it is crimes like this that lubricate the functioning of his kleptocracy.

In spite of enormous efforts by the Russian government, Putin has not been successful at repealing the Magnitsky Act or preventing it from spreading around the world.

However, there is still a lot more that needs to be done, and this is where the Helsinki Commission can act.

First, the number of people sanctioned is woefully inadequate. The U.S. government is in possession of evidence linking at least 282 Russians directly to the Magnitsky case, all of whom should be targeted under the Magnitsky Act. So far, only 35 have been sanctioned. Every December a new Magnitsky sanctions list is published by the U.S. Treasury. I hope this year's list will be robust and responsive to the long backlog of people who still should be sanctioned. I also hope that many other cases of gross human rights abuse in Russia get the attention they deserve.

Second, one of the key perpetrators of the crime that led to Sergei's death, Dmitry Klyuev, appears to be running circles around the U.S. Treasury Department, the agency that enforces the Magnitsky Act. Klyuev was added to the Magnitsky List in 2014 but pre-emptively moved many of his assets into the names of nominees in order to evade sanctions. We've informed the Treasury Department about his alleged sanctions evasion but so far the nominees remain free to manage the assets without consequence. This is an issue that goes well beyond Klyuev.

Third, the rise of Bitcoin and cryptocurrencies will likely create a new way around these sanctions for the Putin regime. As of now, the Magnitsky sanctions are highly effective because once a person is on the Magnitsky list, they become pariahs in the international financial system. The moment a person's name hits the U.S. Treasury sanctions list, no bank in the world wants to do business with that person to avoid being in violation of U.S. sanctions. Unfortunately, Bitcoin and other anonymous cryptocurrencies allow people to bypass the financial system and conduct financial business anonymously. This is an issue which requires the urgent attention of the U.S. and other Western governments in relation to Magnitsky sanctions as well as all other sanctions programs.

Fourth, there is a provision of the Magnitsky Act which requires the U.S. government to encourage other countries to adopt Magnitsky Acts. I believe it should become an explicit U.S. policy to promote the Magnitsky Act at every opportunity.

The next G7 summit will be held in June, 2018, in La Malbaie, Quebec, Canada. This meeting would be an appropriate moment for the U.S. and its partners to advocate for the remaining G7 countries that do not have Magnitsky Acts—Germany, France, Japan and Italy—to adopt their own as soon as possible. More broadly, the U.S. should use its position at the OSCE and the U.N. to further advocate for Magnitsky sanctions around the world.

In conclusion, I'd like to thank the Helsinki Commission for its historic work on the Magnitsky movement and encourage the Commission to double down given the momentum and success of this legislation.

PREPARED STATEMENT OF GARRY KASPAROV, CHAIRMAN, HUMAN
RIGHTS FOUNDATION

Thank you for having me here today, and to Chairman Wicker
and Co-Chairman Smith for holding this hearing on a topic of vital
national and international security.

I will understand if few of you recall that I spoke here over thirteen years ago, in May 2004, on a panel titled "Human Rights in
Putin's Russia." Bill Browder and I were still attempting to do our
part to salvage democracy and the rule of law from inside Putin's
Russia while the entire democratic world preferred to ignore the
true nature of what Putin was doing in my country.

Mikhail Khodorkovsky had just been arrested. There were still a
dwindling handful of Russian media not under Kremlin control.
The Russian parliament still had a few members who would occasionally criticize Putin. Anna Politkovskaya and Boris Nemtsov,
Sergei Magnitsky, and so many others who opposed Putin were all
still alive.

I am not the sort of person to wallow in nostalgia, but it is hard
not to think of how different Russia and the world might be today
had the free world taken a stand against Vladimir Putin back then,
before he had consolidated total power in Russia. In 2004 Putin
still needed friends on the international stage, and he had them.
By 2012 that phase was over, and a far deadlier phase of dictatorship began, when Putin needed not friends, but enemies to justify
his eternal grip on power. Today, there is no longer any need to
discuss human rights in Putin's Russia. They are gone, and Putin
is revealed to all as what we warned he could become: a dictator.

And please, do not speak of Putin's supposed popularity. A popular leader does not need to fake elections, or destroy the free
media, or jail critics or kill opposition leaders. Status that is artificially fashioned by twenty-four-hour propaganda, repression of all
dissent, and the elimination of all rivals is not approval, it is dictatorship. Here, thirteen years ago, I said, "Without Western attention and pressure, the situation will only worsen during Putin's
next four years." We still dreamed that Putin could be forced to
hold real elections in 2008, but it was not to be. Later I said,
"Putin is a Russian problem, for Russians to deal with. But if he
isn't stopped, he will soon be a regional problem—and after that he
will be everyone's problem."

Fast-forward to 2006, and the murder of Russian anti-Putin
whistleblower Alexander Litvinenko in London with a nuclear isotope. To 2008, and Putin's invasion of Georgia—for which he also
suffered no consequences and was even rewarded with the infamous American "Reset." Jump to 2012, and Putin's broad crackdown against any and all opposition and demonstrations, which led
to Boris Nemtsov's murder and my own exile. To 2014, and Putin's
invasion of Crimea and Eastern Ukraine. To 2016, and direct Russian interference in the American presidential election—after similar activities in the UK, Netherlands, and elsewhere in Europe.

For a decade now, many of us familiar with the reality of Putin
and his regime, including both of my fellow guests here to offer testimony, have insisted that the only effective way to pressure Putin
is to target the only thing he cares about: his hold on power in Rus-

sia. And that the best way to target Putin's power is to take aim at his agents and cronies and their money, to pursue the mafia that holds the levers of power and who benefit the most from Putin's rule. The individuals who can influence Putin must be targeted or there can be no effective deterrence. There is no national Russian interest Putin cares about beyond propaganda value. In fact, Russian national interest and Putin's interests are diametrically opposed in nearly every way. Putin does not care about the Russian people, the Russian economy, or the image of Russia abroad. I repeat: he does not care. This is why legislation that targets Putin and his mafia is pro-Russia, not anti-Russia.

But I know that first and foremost we are here to discuss the interests of the United States. Its security, integrity, and economic well-being. Consider the American and other free world policy goals of dealing with Putin's aggression. One, to improve American and international security by deterring him from further hostile acts. Ukraine, Syria, Venezuela, missile tech to North Korea, election meddling—Putin's attacks are asymmetric and so the global response must be asymmetric as well—by going after what matters to him most. Two, to threaten Putin's grasp on total power in Russia by forcing his elites to choose between loyalty to him and their fortunes abroad. Three, to support the long-term interests of the Russian people by exposing the corruption of our rulers. To all three of these goals, the Magnitsky Act is the answer.

Putin's regime is a mafia and you have to fight it like a mafia. Very strong penalties must be ready and widely known. I understand that deterrence is difficult because its fruits are not apparent. If it works, maybe nothing visible happens. To those who say that sanctions have not worked, can you say what else Putin might have done without them in place? Or why he works so frantically to have them repealed?

Progress in a hybrid war is not measured in territory conquered or battlefield casualties. Corrupting influence and propaganda spread like a contagious disease. You can measure the effectiveness of the Magnitsky legislation the way you measure the effectiveness of antibiotics. You put a drop in the petri dish and see if the bacteria stop growing, if the bacteria respond to the antibiotic and die. By this measure, the Magnitsky Act has been effective, and could be much more effective if strengthened and implemented globally and aggressively.

Last month, a Reuters report said anxiety was spreading among Russia's wealthiest because of sanctions and the threat of the U.S. blacklist. It reported that some business leaders were trying to avoid being seen in public near Putin, and to distance themselves. This is progress; it shows the medicine is effective. But anxiety is not enough to turn against a brutal dictator. Avoiding photo ops is not enough to bring down a mafia. It is essential to increase the pressure, to continue with what works now that the right path has been confirmed. There is no other method.

Putin's weapons of hybrid war can only be defended against at great difficulty and expense. Misinformation, cyberwarfare, and other methods are cheap and easy to deploy, and—take it from a pretty good chessplayer—playing only defense is always a losing game. The answer is deterrence. Putin and his gang must understand that, if he continues this path, their fortunes, their families' comfortable lives abroad, will be at risk. They aren't jihadists or ideologues, they are billionaires who are used to profiting from dictatorship at home while enjoying the good life in the West. End that perverse double standard. Follow the money, the real estate, the stock, and reveal it, freeze it, so that one day it can be returned to the Russian people from whom it was looted, and to help rebuild the country that has been drained for two decades. The brittle nature of Putin's one-man dictatorship will be exposed very quickly.

The alternative to appeasement is not war, it is deterrence. And worrying about retaliation is absurd when Putin will continue to escalate anyway, as long as he thinks he can get away with it. The best way to avoid an escalating conflict is to convince your opponent that he will lose. And make no mistake, there is a war going on whether you want to admit it or not. It is very easy to lose a war that you refuse to acknowledge even exists. Engagement has failed because Putin was never your friend. There is no common ground. Now he has revealed his true colors as a sworn enemy of the free world. And time is of the essence.

Thank you.

About Garry Kasparov—Garry Kasparov is widely regarded as the greatest chessplayer in history, becoming the youngest world champion ever at 22 in 1985. He retired in 2005 to become a leader of the Russian pro-democracy movement against the rising dictatorship of Vladimir Putin. He is the chairman of the New York-based Human Rights Foundation and is a powerful voice for individual freedom worldwide. In 2015, he wrote the prescient book "Winter Is Coming: Why Putin and the Enemies of the Free World Must Be Stopped." His latest is "Deep Thinking: Where Machine Intelligence Ends and Human Creativity Begins" (2017).

For further information: Mig Greengard, senior aide to Garry Kasparov   mgreengard@kasparov.com   office@kasparov.com +1 917.495.9460

PREPARED STATEMENT OF IRWIN COTLER, PC, OC, CHAIR, RAOUL WALLENBERG CENTER FOR HUMAN RIGHTS

I am delighted to participate in the common cause which brings us together—the struggle against the cultures of criminality and corruption and the impunity that underpins them—and this as part of the larger pursuit of justice and accountability both domestically and internationally.

We meet at an important moment of remembrance and reminder:

- The 8th anniversary of the torture and murder of Sergei Magnitsky—who uncovered the largest corporate tax fraud in Russian history and paid for it with his life—and where in a move that would make Kafka blush, the Russians engaged in a posthumous prosecution of Magnitsky for the very fraud that he had exposed.

- The 5th anniversary of the adoption here in the U.S. of the Sergei Magnitsky Rule of Law Accountability Act, which inspired similar initiatives elsewhere.

- The immediate aftermath of the unanimous adoption by both houses of the Canadian Parliament of Global Justice for Sergei Magnitsky legislation, titled "Justice for Victims of Corrupt Foreign Officials Act."

Accordingly, what I would like to do is first, summarize briefly the process in Canada—as a matter of chronology and content—that led to this historic, albeit belated, Canadian initiative; Second, summarize the raison d'etre of this legislation; and finally some brief comments and where do we go from here, in Canada and internationally.

First, having regard to the genesis and development of the Magnitsky process, it was inspired, not unlike the U.S., by an encounter I had with Bill Browder in 2010 in the UK, and which led to the launch of the Justice for Sergei Magnitsky movement in Canada. A series of initiatives in November 2010 alone provide a looking glass into the character and content of the movement, which included:

- Meeting of the Foreign Affairs Subcommittee on International Human Rights with Bill Browder as principal witness on November 2nd

- International parliamentary premiere of "Justice for Sergei Magnitsky" documentary

- First of many Op-Eds calling for Justice for Sergei Magnitsky and outlining the advocacy and legislative framework to be followed

- Unanimous adoption by the Foreign Affairs Subcommittee of my motion calling, inter alia, for justice for Sergei Magnitsky legislation modeled on the U.S. initiative.

One year later, I introduced a private Member's Bill titled "an Act to Condemn Corruption and Impunity in Russia in the Case and Death of Sergei Magnitsky," the first legislative initiative of its kind in the Canadian Parliament, but being from an opposition party it required support from the government of the day, which was not forthcoming.

In 2012, Boris Nemtsov, leading Russian democrat, came to Canada to support this Private Member's Bill along with Vladimir Kara-Murza, and later that year we launched the Justice for Sergei Magnitsky Interparliamentary Group, which led to resolutions being adopted in the European Parliament and country adoptions in Estonia and Lithuania.

In 2013 the pattern of unanimous motions continued, but the focus now shifted to representations to the Canadian Government, and where Bill Browder and I joined in meetings with Government Ministers, and where we conveyed documentary evidence of the criminality and corruption of sixty Russian officials, but our efforts to get Government actions were unavailing. The year 2014 began with Canada sanctioning Russian officials for Russian aggression re: Crimea and the Ukraine, and with Russia retaliating by banning 13 Canadian leaders, including MP Chrystia Freeland (who was later to become Minister of Foreign Affairs) and myself, but still no government legislation re: Magnitsky.

2015 witnessed a number of dramatic developments, which began to move us in the direction of legislation.

- In February 2015 Boris Nemtsov, leading campaigner internationally for Justice for Sergei Magnitsky legislation and a leading critic of Russian aggression in Crimea and Ukraine, was murdered just outside the Kremlin.

- In March 2015 the House unanimously adopted my motion calling for Global Justice for Sergei Magnitsky legislation again inspired by the developments in the U.S.

- In June I introduced, again as a Private Member's Bill, the Global Magnitsky Human Rights Accountability Act and while the Conservative Government finally agreed to adopt the legislation, the process was adjourned by the calling of an election.

- In the course of the election, each of the three principal political parties, Liberals, Conservatives, and the New Democratic Parties committed themselves to adopting such legislation if elected.

- The Liberal Party won the election but the momentum of the Government was stalled. The new Foreign Minister Stephane Dion, considering that such legislation was unnecessary (i.e. we had other domestic legislation which would suffice) and that it would prejudice our "re-engagement with Russia."

Accordingly, we reignited the parliamentary process—now in both Houses—and again with the witness testimony of Bill Browder, Vladimir Kara-Murza, Zhanna Nemtsova, and Garry Kasparov. A number of developing factors underpinned the momentum, including:

- The founding of the All-Party Raoul Wallenberg Parliamentary Caucus for Human Rights, which made such legislation a priority

- Unanimous report from the Foreign Affairs Committee calling for Global Justice for Sergei Magnitsky legislation

- The leadership of the newly appointed Foreign Minister Chrystia Freeland, who in May 2017 announced Government support for Sergei Magnitsky Global Justice and Accountability legislation

- Succession of Russian threats emanating both from the Russian embassy in Canada and Putin himself warning against Canadian

adoption of that legislation and the adverse impact it would have on Canada-Russia relations
- Meeting of the Raoul Wallenberg Caucus calling not only for the passage of the legislation, but for its unanimous adoption, so as to send a message to the Kremlin that we will not be intimidated
- Finally, Global Justice for Sergei Magnitsky legislation passes unanimously in both Houses and received royal assent

The momentum for the legislation was not unrelated to the resurgent global authoritarianism, which mandated a Global Human Rights Act, because while Russia was a major human rights violator—arguably the most threatening of the human rights violators because of its externalized aggression and its domestic repression—Russia was not the only human rights violator, which accounted therefore for the objectives and purposes which underpin this legislation and which includes:

First, to combat the persistent and pervasive culture of corruption, criminality, and impunity.

Second, to deter thereby other would-be or prospective violators, because if we indulge that culture of impunity, we only embolden the human rights violators. If we sanction the human rights violators, we can deter others because they know there is a price to be paid for their corruption or criminality.

Third is that we make the pursuit of international justice a priority and a pillar of our human rights policy both domestic and international.

The fourth is to uphold the rule of law and justice and accountability in our own territory through visa bans and asset seizures and the like. The recent evidence of how Magnitsky assets have been laundered in Canada is but one case study of the importance of having this type of comprehensive legislation.

Fifth, this legislation does not interfere with the sovereignty of any other country. We are not acting in any other country. What we are seeking to do is to protect our own sovereignty, our own rule of law, our own economy, and to exclude these would-be perpetrators from exercising what is in effect a privilege, and not a right, to enter our country.

Sixth, is to protect Canadian businesses operating abroad. Magnitsky uncovered the largest corporate tax fraud in Russian history, which was perpetrated against a U.K.-based entity, Hermitage Capital, so this type of legislation would protect not only the integrity of commerce in Canada, but also our Canadian businessmen operating abroad.

Seventh, is the importance of the naming and shaming of human rights violators, so that they cannot, in effect, leverage their culture of criminality and corruption to come to Canada, purchase houses here, vacation here, send their children to schools here, launder their assets here, and the like. In other words, we need to protect the integrity of our sovereignty, our rule of law, our economy, and our institutions.

Eighth, it is important to appreciate that this legislation targets human rights violators and not governments, targeting individuals who have engaged in gross violation of internationally recognized human rights such as extrajudicial executions, torture, widespread and systematic targeting of civilians, and to prevent them from entering our country or laundering their assets here.

Ninth, such legislation would not bind the Canadian government; rather, it would empower the Canadian government. It would allow us to be a protector of human rights, and not an enabler of the violators of human rights.

Finally, and most importantly, it tells the human rights defenders, the Magnitskys of today in Russia or those in any other part of the world, such as Raif Badawi in Saudi Arabia or Leopoldo López in Venezuela or the Baha'i in Iran, that they are not alone, that we stand in solidarity with them, that we will not relent in our pursuit of justice for them, and that we will undertake our international responsibilities in the pursuit of justice and in the combatting of the culture of impunity and criminality in these respective countries.

Where do we go from here? May I make a number of suggestions:

First, we should seek to internationalize the Global Justice for Sergei Magnitsky movement and secure as many participating countries as possible. As Boris Nemtsov put it, the adoption of Magnitsky legislation by EU countries would be a serious blow to the criminal regime in Russia. As he put it, "If you want to protect yourself against Putin's thieves, murderers, and corrupt officials, you must adopt the Magnitsky law."

Second, three of the G7 countries have now adopted Magnitsky legislation—the U.S., UK, Canada—as Canada assumes the presidency of the G7—and the next G7 meeting will be held in Quebec—we should seek to mobilize support for such legislation in the four remaining G7 countries—Germany, France, Italy, and Japan.

Third, we need to make the OSCE a focal point of our advocacy for Justice for Sergei Magnitsky legislation, anchored in our commitments under the Helsinki Final Act, where the OSCE countries have affirmed that "issues relating to human rights, fundamental freedoms, democracy, and the rule of law, are of international concern and the respect of these rights and freeedoms constitutes one of the foundations of the international order. Therefore we have not only a right but a responsibility to hold Russia—an OSCE state—accountable for the standing violation of its commitments.

Fourth, the assault on human rights and the rule of law—and the imprisonment of human rights defenders—is a standing violation of principle seven of the Helsinki Final Act—the right of people to know and act upon their rights, and here too, Russia must be held accountable re: its political prisoners.

Fifth, from a global perspective, Global Justice for Sergei Magnitsky legislation should combat the resurgent global authoritarianism—and the culture of impunity that underpins it—by sanctioning human rights violators, be they in Russia, Venezuela, or South Sudan, which is something Canada has done since our adoption of the legislation. In the end of the day, in adopting Magnitsky legislation we make a statement not only of what we must do, but of who we are.

MATERIAL FOR THE RECORD

COVER OF THE CANADIAN PARLIAMENT FOREIGN AFFAIRS COMMITTEE REPORT, APRIL 2017

This is an official publication of the
**Commission on Security and
Cooperation in Europe.**

★ ★ ★

This publication is intended to document
developments and trends in participating
States of the Organization for Security
and Cooperation in Europe (OSCE).

★ ★ ★

All Commission publications may be freely
reproduced, in any form, with appropriate
credit. The Commission encourages
the widest possible dissemination
of its publications.

★ ★ ★

http://www.csce.gov   @HelsinkiComm

The Commission's Web site provides
access to the latest press releases
and reports, as well as hearings and
briefings. Using the Commission's electronic
subscription service, readers are able
to receive press releases, articles,
and other materials by topic or countries
of particular interest.

Please subscribe today.